D0498137

THE TRANSFORMATIONS OF GODOT

THE TRANSFORMATIONS OF
GODOT

Frederick Busi

WITH A FOREWORD BY WYLIE SYPHER

THE UNIVERSITY PRESS OF KENTUCKY

ISBN: 0-8131-1392-X

Library of Congress Catalog Card Number: 79-4002

Copyright © 1980 by The University Press of Kentucky

Scholarly publisher for the Commonwealth,
serving Berea College, Centre College of Kentucky,
Eastern Kentucky University, The Filson Club,
Georgetown College, Kentucky Historical Society,
Kentucky State University, Morehead State University,
Murray State University, Northern Kentucky University,
Transylvania University, University of Kentucky,
University of Louisville, and Western Kentucky University.

Editorial and Sales Offices: Lexington, Kentucky 40506

To my wife, Esta, with love and gratitude

"When I use a word," Humpty Dumpty said, in a rather scornful tone," it means just what I choose it to mean — neither more nor less."

"The question is," said Alice, "whether you can make words mean so many different things."

"The question is," said Humpty Dumpty, "which is to be master — that's all."

LEWIS CARROLL

The kind of work I do is one in which I'm not master of my material. The more Joyce knew the more he could. He's tending toward omniscience and omnipotence as an artist. I'm working with impotence, ignorance.

SAMUEL BECKETT

CONTENTS

FOREWORD

This discussion of Beckett's most-analysed drama extends and
refines interpretations which have not been fully explored in
the mass of existing commentary on *Godot:* the role of the
clown and Harlequin, and the transforming of the "double"
in the play-within-the-play, Beckett's relation to the commedia dell'arte, to Cervantes, to Joyce's punning technique,
to mythology, to apocryphal tradition, to the particular
tyranny implicit in the character of Pozzo, and above all
to the significance of stage names. But it would be wrong
to take this book as a mere study of influences on Beckett,
for Busi has examined the very nature and operation of
Beckett's art not only in the theater but also in fiction.
And Busi is intelligent, informed, and sensitive enough
to recognize that his innovative readings of *Godot* are not
the only ones available.

This book is of value to anyone concerned with either
Beckett or Joyce. Even when some of Busi's findings are
conjectural (as he indicates), they are illuminating and pro-
vocative. Busi has the advantage of familiarity with the
psychological implications of the play, especially regarding
schizophrenia and modern self-deception. Yet he is not
offering a bleak, oversimplified clinical analysis. The book
is an invitation to expand our reading of Beckett in many
directions, notably about the cryptic figure of Pozzo, concerning whom there has been so much speculation. Busi

identifies in Beckett a range of hermetic apocryphal doc-
trines tracing back to Marcion and Gnosticism.

Throughout, Busi is aware of the art form in which Beckett
is working, and he specifies the differences between Joyce's
linguistic exercises and Beckett's spare dramaturgy, which
is likewise rooted in etymology, myth, and the Dublin milieu.
As Busi's examination progresses, he involves the major
themes of the play-within-the-play and how the hat trick
in the doubles recurs, finally focusing on Pozzo as a secular
Messiah and as an intermediary of the mutable self. Busi's
formidable learning in these areas demonstrates how Beckett
modified and enriched Joyce's arcane methods and materials.

Thus Busi clarifies and consolidates meanings sometimes
previously noted by such Beckett critics as Ruby Cohn, Hugh
Kenner, John Fletcher, Vivian Mercier, Sighle Kennedy, and
Lawrence Harvey. This book should enlighten all those who
are curious about modern dramaturgy, and it affords the
specialists in Beckett, Joyce, and Cervantes a firmly ground-
ed, stimulating view of Beckett's oblique art and Joyce's
fictional techniques.

Wylie Sypher
Simmons College

ACKNOWLEDGMENTS

A grant from the Graduate Research Council of the University of Massachusetts, Amherst, enabled me to write this book. For helping me in the preparation of the manuscript special thanks are due to Professors Eric Beekman, Bernard Elevitch, Henry Grosshans, Sighle Kennedy, Henri Peyre, Jules Piccus, Irving Rothberg, Wylie Sypher, and to my wife, Esta. To all I am indebted.

Permission to quote from Beckett's works has been kindly granted by Editions de Minuit for *En Attendant Godot* and Grove Press for *Waiting for Godot*. All quotations in this study have been taken from these editions.

1. Introduction

> Let us sit on this anthill for our frilldress talk after
> this day of making blithe inveiled the heart before
> our groatsupper serves to us Panchomaster and let
> harleqwind play peeptomine up all our colombina-
> tions! Wins won is nought, twigs too is nil, tricks
> trees makes nix, fairs fears stoops at nothing.
> JAMES JOYCE

> Unless the names are known to you,
> The concepts will be hazy too.
> LINNAEUS

This book is designed to fill a gap in Beckett studies. It is not another general study of *Waiting for Godot;* it is a specialized book that focuses on the significance of onomastic techniques employed by Samuel Beckett in his masterpiece. The questions I ask are simple although the answers are complicated and, I hope, stimulating and revealing. In his work *Of Grammatology* Jacques Derrida has a chapter called "The Battle of Proper Names." These words could easily serve as the subtitle to my study, which attempts to shed some light on the names of Didi, Gogo, Pozzo, and Lucky.

These names cannot be studied in total isolation, to the neglect of related considerations. Their analysis means much more than tracing etymological derivations; it requires detailed examination of associated dramatic themes. It is to these tasks that the bulk of this study is devoted. The bizarre names of Beckett's four main characters stand out in contrast against the bone-dry landscape of *Waiting for Godot*.

This facet of their roles has received little sustained comment from most critics. The character names were not inserted for the discernment of clever readers: they serve, linguistically, profound dramatic functions intended to reinforce the changing roles assumed by Beckett's characters.

In analyzing these names my central purpose is to show how Beckett, through the names he chooses, suggests that his two tramps, in waiting for Godot, are really waiting for themselves. In the shape of Pozzo he is already present among them and they do not know it. More important, they do not wish to know it. Beckett has stated that "self-perception is the most frightening of all human observations . . ."[1] The playwright's character names are intimately bound to this tortuous quest and avoidance of the self, a selfhood which many critics have found to be lacking or at least very elusive in this play.

The Pozzo-Godot equation has been considered by a few critics and dismissed by many more, but this connection is more involved than any of them may have suspected. The genealogy runs straight through to Gogo and has profound implications for his relationship to his companion, Didi. Who is really the slave of whom? Analysis of their family trees should help to answer this question.

To demonstrate the point I have examined Beckett's technique of character naming from four perspectives, using an approach that is largely comparative. I begin by considering Beckett's affinities with Cervantes and the indebtedness of both authors to the tradition of the commedia dell'arte and the figure of Harlequin, with special emphasis on the notion of interchangeable character roles. The chapters that follow contain detailed discussions of Beckett's use of the play-within-a-play as a dramatic device, his debt to James Joyce, and the significance and ramifications of those religious and psychological themes which bear upon the development of the self. My critical range is admittedly broad, but these investigations all converge on Beckett's handling of names. In his sphere of creativity language, words, and names are ultimately central to his dramatic concerns. It has been observed quite often that Beckett's objective is a "literature of the Unword" in which language disintegrates, "until that which lurks behind it . . . begins to trickle through."[2] The various associations conjured up by the names will serve to reinforce this general observation in Beckett's creative endeavor.

Despite its apparent structural simplicity, *Waiting for Godot* is suffused with a densely suggestive vision. Hugh Kenner describes the work in terms of "its eloquence spare then, still spare now, yet positively garrulous by the standards he sets himself today."[3] This eloquent garrulity is the subject of my study. I have placed particular emphasis upon the way in which characters' names perform for Beckett the dramatic and psychological functions of representing the multiple aspects of personality transformation insofar as they are related to themes that hold special appeal for the author. Throughout, I have also attempted on a secondary level to trace the development of the clown as a major figure in character growth, attesting to Beckett's abiding confidence in the imagination and his limitless skill in creating new dramatic shapes and contexts for his craft.

In literature, names often denote character traits. But because Beckett's names are so unusual, character analysis is difficult to achieve. One problem with writing about Beckett is that he is often reluctant to elucidate his own works. He is not reticent, on the other hand, about denying various interpretations attributed to his creations. "The first principle of criticism," writes Pope in the postscript to his translation of the *Odyssey*, "is to consider the nature of the piece, and the intent of the author." In Beckett's case the task is far from simple. He speaks with the testy sibylline clairvoyance of Humpty Dumpty. When Alan Schneider, the first American producer of *Waiting for Godot,* asked him what *Godot* meant he answered: "If I knew, I would have said so in the play."[4] Similarly, when Alice dared to put a question to Humpty Dumpty he replied: "If I'd meant that, I'd have said it." Like Lewis Carroll and James Joyce, Samuel Beckett betrays a fondness for verbal ambiguity, puns, and portmanteau words. Like these two authors he demands much from this linguistic technique in order subtly to express his genius and befuddle his readers.[5]

Alec Reid reports that "during a conversation in 1956 Beckett made one very illuminating remark to the effect that the great success of *Waiting for Godot* had arisen from a misunderstanding; critics and public alike, he said, were seeking to impose an allegorical or symbolic explanation on a play which was striving all the time to avoid definition."[6] Because of such warnings many critics have tended to shy away from too explicit evaluations of details encountered in this play, focusing instead upon the playwright's lean style and his supposed radical pessimism. One of the aims of this study will be to show how Beckett has deliberately incorporated into his play a treatment of symbols and character development that precludes any static interpretations.

But that fundamental problem remains. If Beckett denies explanations of symbols, why did he put them into his play? All critics have observed his numerous references to Christian symbols, but there is no common agreement concerning their purpose. An analysis of *Waiting for Godot* from the perspective of onomastic techniques would show, I believe, that Beckett's Spartan dialogue is deceptively rich and mainly devised to emphasize the basic conflicting unity of his two pairs of clowns. Didi and Gogo, and Lucky and Pozzo, are the changing masks of the same personality. They are all one and the same creature engaged in a monologue with the mutable, elusive self.

Close scrutiny of character names, and hence character functions and traits, enables the reader to appreciate another closely related feature of the play: these individuals are not really waiting for some person named Godot, because Godot is already present among them. They are, as Alain Robbe-Grillet parenthetically observed, waiting for themselves.[7] But how and why, the French critic-novelist does not tell us. A careful examination of their names should help provide some insight regarding their activities.

Ever since Martin Esslin wrote that "the subject of the play is not Godot but waiting," most critics have reacted to the drama by chanting various jeremiads on the fate of humanity.[8] Esslin's stricture may be well taken, but the aim of this book is to show that Beckett did not intend to divorce Godot from the waiting. The function of Godot, and to a lesser extent, his identity, is intimately bound up with the theme of waiting as a form of messianic expectation with all that this implies in the history of religion and theater. Beckett once wrote that "form *is* content, content *is* form."[9] The two cannot be separated without doing violence to the basic unity of this play.

The problem with stressing Godot is that those critics who have done so flatly assert that Godot was modeled on, among others, a character from Balzac, a French bicycle rider, or the image of a God who never appears. None of these assertions really does credit to Beckett's genius. If Beckett wished only to reflect human despair before a disappearing and disappointing deity, then he would be nothing more than the village atheist turned playwright. The play undoubtedly owes too much of its success to this misconception on the public's part, and Beckett is justified in disassociating himself from such an interpretation. Growing popularization of the "death of God" theology and of various forms of existentialism probably reinforced this view of the work. The play does have something to do with religion but not in the way many critics and the public have often assumed. This aspect of the piece will be discussed in detail in the third chapter.

That note of radical despair which typifies much discussion

of the play revolves round a peculiar brand of nihilism frequently associated with Beckett. He is truly the poet of the void and has realized Flaubert's wish to write a book about nothing. One critic, Vivian Mercier, described *Waiting for Godot* as a play where "nothing happens — *twice.*" Its opening line, "Nothing to be done," can suggest positive as well as negative dimensions to the attentive reader. Beckett's clowns have a lot of nothing to do, and most of this nothingness is voiced with words.

Like Wittgenstein, Beckett is well aware of the dangerous charms of language. For this reason he makes one of his characters, Malone, observe with a nod to Democritus: "I know those little phrases that seem so innocuous and, once you let them in, pollute the whole of speech. *Nothing is more real than nothing.* They rise up out of the pit and know no rest until they drag you down into its dark. But I am on my guard now."[10] While he is the master of esoteric nonsense when he wishes to be, Beckett is constantly paring down his language, mindful of its bewitching appeal. In terms of his total achievement Beckett's career can be generally divided into three phases: the early years reflected the Joycean influence, and the later ones bear witness to a radical streamlining of language; the middle years, however, during which *Godot* was written, will probably remain uppermost in the minds of the vast public. At this creative watershed Beckett was able to incorporate elements that suggest the opposing aesthetic currents of the early and later periods. In *Waiting for Godot* these tendencies are struggling with one another. For this reason alone a detailed study of certain features of its language is warranted. However convoluted and fanciful his early work may have been, he was always striving to express and reflect the various dimensions of the void. And as late as *Godot* the playwright had not yet abandoned his rich command of language in the form of concrete symbols. Here, too, proper names under greater control generate conflict and stimulate the imagination.

Beckett, the poet of the void, nevertheless realizes the practical necessity of artistic creativity, of producing something even if it is supposed to represent the passage of human inactivity and vacuity. In the same year that *Godot* was first staged, Beckett published *Watt* and expressed a pragmatic compromise in the conflict between form and content: "For the only way one can speak of nothing is to speak of it as though it were something, just as the only way one can speak of God is to speak of him as though he were a man, which to be sure he was, in a sense, for a time, and as the only way one can speak of man, even our anthropologists have realised that, is to speak of him as though he were a termite."[11] It is of this kind of nothingness that Beckett humorously sings. It gives his masterpiece additional perspective and demands respect for his sensitivity to language. No matter how often the play is read or seen it still leaves the beholder with the nagging impression that the characters' overt inactivity is accompanied by some covert, unspecified purposiveness. The goal of this study is to recognize these elements and to trace their dramatic development and functions through Beckett's manipulation of onomastic devices.

A longtime friend of Beckett, A. J. Leventhal, wrote that "there is a certain esoteric quality hidden skeletally in Beckett's work."[12] Such a view should be balanced by awareness of the author's penchant for intriguing and then chiding his audience.[13] In order to appreciate the critical approach which I present in this book the reader is urged to consider a remarkable work to which I am indebted, *Murphy's Bed*, by Sighle Kennedy. This study is a detailed analysis of the arcane material found in Beckett's novel, *Murphy*. To similar elements in *Waiting for Godot* I address myself in this book. I make no claims to unlock all the mysteries of Godot. Plays so easily analysed just are not interesting plays.

My critical approach is basically philological and comparative because the study of language is germane to the appreciation of literature and is apt to disclose the obscure sources

and functions of the play under discussion. I have attempted
to stay close to the text, to pursue and investigate only those
key concepts and symbols that Beckett has seen fit to use and
transform. Here I am reminded of Molloy's statement: "All I
know is what the words know."[14] And with Beckett the words
know a great deal, especially the ones not found in dictionaries.

Character names have to do with the unfolding of the self.
And with Beckett the self is often perceived to be schizoid.
This theme has already been partly explored by various
critics, many of whose works smack a bit too much of the
casebook variety of analysis. But it must be remembered
that Beckett is not a psychologist, philosopher, or theologian:
he is above all an artist and language is his only means and
end. My claim to originality in this study is the attention I
bring to bear on Beckett's linguistic development of the
schizoid self as revealed through character names. In Beckett's
hands his characters' personalities are forever disintegrating
and reforming and dissolving again, and their multiple names
help tell this story.[15]

In this study my examination of Beckett's language has
also been influenced by the works of Leo Spitzer and Roland
Barthes. I am indebted to the former's profound grasp of
philology in microscopically analysing the particularities
of the literary text and to the latter's hermeneutics. For
Barthes meaning is multiple; he is concerned with the perpetual present and inventive interplay of language that yield
a plurality of readings and reactions.[16]

Beckett has inherited and transformed the Symbolist
aesthetics of contrived ambiguity. But with Beckett in particular it is not so much a question of multiple meanings as
such. As he himself has stated, *Waiting for Godot* is a play
"striving to avoid definition." Its various interwoven elements draw close and then lead away from one another. The
critic and reader should be concerned not with any ultimate
significance discovered in the text but rather with its various

voices and resonances, each yielding to an imaginative and animating multiplication of the symbols and words themselves. The play was meant to be seen on stage and to be read as a book. It is a palimpsest that grants many rewards to the diligent audience.

Conversely, it should also be remembered that this play need not always be treated as a ouija board or as Vivian Mercier puts it "a sort of living Rorschach test."[17] It fulfills these functions and many more. Through the use of specific symbols and dramatic techniques the author has established a certain pattern, however protean, which permits critical discussion along the guidelines set forth below. My critical interest in this play was revived by Melvin Friedman's comment that "not much has been said about the modest play-within-a-play in *Godot*."[18] It is one of my intentions to demonstrate in each chapter that this dramatic device as used by Beckett will reveal the interrelationship between his characters in terms of their role exchanges. Above all I have been guided by the same sense of wonder experienced by Roger Blin who, after hearing some of Beckett's poetry, remembered "being struck by the complexity of thought expressed in the simplicity of the language."[19] His theater is no less rewarding.

In this study the theme of character development will be examined from four distinct though related perspectives, with emphasis on the significance of the characters' names. The second chapter deals with the impact of the commedia dell'arte and its clowns upon Cervantes and Beckett. The third chapter analyses the techniques of the play-within-a-play and polyglot punning and how their use by Shakespeare and above all by Joyce was developed and adapted by Beckett for his own dramatic intentions. The fourth chapter also pursues this line of investigation with stress on the religious and mythological symbols that help to elucidate Beckett's handling of names. Thus the main question posed by this study remains: Why did Beckett give those particular names to his characters?

In order to avoid any initial misunderstanding, it should again be stated that this is not a general examination of Beckett's play: there are already enough studies available which fill that need. Throughout these chapters I have tried to discuss in my crabwise fashion certain features of *Godot* as a work of art and secondarily to relate its connection to specific themes in European theater and thought.

Unlike that Dante whom he admired, Beckett has written no letter to a modern Can Grande della Scala to explain the four dimensions, the literal, moral, allegorical, and anagogical aspects, of his works. Yet these dimensions in modern form and others are all present in Beckett's creation. Like Beckett, I, too, am interested in the shape of things and ideas. And while he is more taken with the shape than with the ideas as such, certain patterns of thought are nonetheless present and they contribute to the dynamic structure and impact of the play.

Those who wish to appreciate my critical approach should ponder the quotation from James Joyce which I have chosen as the epigraph for this introduction. Almost all that I have to say in this book is to be found in this apostrophe about Cervantes. I have done no more than to comment on what Joyce's genius was able to reduce to two sentences and how such sensitivity to language was developed and transformed by his disciple Samuel Beckett.

2. The Rebirths of Harlequin

But, Sin Showpanza, could anybroddy which walked
this world with eyes whiteopen have looked twinsomer
than the kerl he left behind him?

JAMES JOYCE

The figure of the clown is a highly fitting vehicle for conveying the onomastic development of Beckett's characters. His
masks and protean nature are suitable for expressing the
unfolding of the elusive self throughout its wanderings between knowledge and ignorance. Before considering Beckett's
clowns' names there is the question of their origins. These
buffoons have been compared with a spectrum of types.
Considering the narrative frame of *Waiting for Godot*, perhaps the clowns described by critic Paul Jennings come closest to resembling what Beckett was trying to express on the
stage: "There was that wonderful troupe of acrobats, with
doleful Edwardian moustaches and long thin shorts, who
filled the stage of the Palladium with endless preparation
and cries of 'Hup!' and never actually did anything."[1]

Beckett's own clowns seem to be garbed in the costumes
of Edwardian music hall comedians and there is every reason
to assume that he was familiar with such vaudeville types
during his early years. Like the practitioners of this slapstick
tradition his clowns wear costumes that suggest a certain
shabby genteel air, one that indicates they might have seen
better days and that their personalities are anchored as much
in the past as in the present. The image of his buffoons, however, is not limited to this century.

The two clowns from *Waiting for Godot* have been fleetingly compared with the clowns of the commedia dell'arte and those of Cervantes. Didi and Gogo may be dressed like modern clowns but their genealogy goes directly back to the time of Cervantes and even before. In fact the masterworks of Cervantes and Beckett owe much to the spirit and characters of the Italian comic tradition of the sixteenth century.[2] Not much attention, however, has been paid to this similarity. Nevertheless its presence permeates *Don Quixote* and *Waiting for Godot* to the extent that a comparison is justifiable in order to examine the onomastic techniques employed by both authors. The two creative works are linked by a wealth of secondary details and, more important, by their common theme of interchangeable character parts. Since the family tree of Beckett's fools goes back to the Italian and Spanish traditions, the best place to begin analysis of their names would be with the work of Cervantes.

At the beginning of modern European literature there stands and remains one of the greatest novels of all — *Don Quixote*. It is not surprising that contemporary critics have discovered in it the precursors of what has been termed antiliterature with particular reference to the works of Beckett. In a pertinent article on *Godot,* John Moore writes that one may view "Gogo and Didi as distant (perhaps the last) descendants of Don Quixote and Sancho Panza."[3] Although there is no categorical proof of Cervantes's influence on Beckett, it would be unthinkable that one of this century's major novelists was unfamiliar with the masterpiece created by that genre's principal developer.[4] It would be as if one said that Beckett had not read the Bible. The clowns of Cervantes and Beckett exhibit across the centuries a type of naïve, pathetic patience in the face of renewed disappointments, and their names bear witness to common designs.

Much has already been written about Beckett's creations as examples of antiliterature, and it would be pointless here

to pursue once again this aspect of his work.[5] What may be
more instructive is an examination of his masterpiece and of
Cervantes's, in order to reveal profound similarities and to
evaluate their impacts, with Cervantes standing at the beginning and Beckett at what has become fashionable to term
the end of modern Western civilization and literature. Those
critics who link Cervantes, along with Furetière, Swift, and
Sterne, to Beckett have done so in rather general terms. It
would, therefore, be profitable to subject both Cervantes's
and Beckett's chief creations to a closer examination for the
purpose of disclosing the deeper links that unite them in matters of theme, detail, myth, and intentions. The two works
bear evidence of similar circumstances in plot and design.
But on a more important level it is the authors' treatment
of the relationship between master and slave that retains
our attention. Once this theme is established, it will become
evident that Beckett and Cervantes have in their respective
works created elaborate, complex portrayals of the monodrama wherein the principal characters exchange roles. Their
onomastic imaginations are no less formidable.

There exists between Beckett and Cervantes a thread of
relationship, a genealogy of design and purpose. Hugh Kenner
writes: "For Beckett is the heir of Joyce as Joyce is the heir
of Flaubert."[6] Kenner could have added that Flaubert is the
heir of Cervantes. Madame Bovary has rightly been described
as a female Don Quixote, her mind glutted by romantic books
just as the knight's was by books about chivalry. And just as
Flaubert memorized entire passages of Cervantes, so Joyce
committed to memory many of Flaubert's best pages. This
lineage seems a bit tenuous but the pervasive influence of
Cervantes is present nonetheless. The Spaniard's parodic
fiction opened new possibilities in the development of characterization and literary psychology. Just as he parodies the
effects of books on chivalry, so Flaubert parodies the impact
of romantic literature, Joyce travesties the *Odyssey,* and

Beckett writes a burlesque on the biblical myth of redemption.[7]

It is neither surprising nor regrettable that Cervantes's work continues to engender so many conflicting interpretations and responses far beyond its creator's declared intentions, for as Erich Auerbach observes: "A book like *Don Quixote* dissociates itself from its author's intention and leads a life of its own."[8] Judging by the bulk and quality of criticism on Beckett, his work is traveling down a similar path and for the same reason.

While it is often rewarding to compare two artists, it is also difficult when they belong to different cultures and historical periods. Yet where there is sufficient compelling evidence to justify such an undertaking, the critic should proceed with caution and circumspection. He would be well advised to practice the discretion of an Américo Castro, for example, in his illuminating article on the possible influences of Cervantes on Pirandello. Castro believes that the Italian probably did not consciously intend to use the same themes and techniques as Cervantes; however, the latter's unmistakable imprint is to be found in Pirandello's work.[9] What unites these two artists is their particular yet similar handling of the conflict between reality and illusion.[10]

Beckett's work also bears an uncanny resemblance to that of Cervantes, for in both cases the main characters are hard pressed to distinguish their perceptions from the stimuli, to draw objective connections between what they experience and what they wish to experience. It is precisely this dislocation of judgment which allows different voices to speak in the same language and in the same passages. In this confusion the characters from both works even exchange roles, thus confirming the thesis that they are really multiple aspects of the same personality.[11]

The major characters of Cervantes's and Beckett's chief works are, above all, clowns. They may be variously described as wanderers, Everyman figures, servants, or even tramps, but ultimately their identities and actions bear the stamp of the buffoon. Not merely in the matter of their playfulness, mock-seriousness, or tendency toward improvisation, but also in their particular conduct one can discover the source and animations of their deeds and dreams in the Italian commedia.

This observation should not imply that both creations are exclusively inspired by Italian sources, but it is noteworthy that their authors have given strong evidence of such influence. Beckett, for example, shows a distinct taste for miming throughout his works. And Cervantes was quite familiar with contemporary Italian culture, especially the theater.[12] Of greater significance is the similarity of function between characters like Pierrot and Sancho, and Harlequin and Don Quixote. Pierrot, in the early stages of his dramatic evolution, was a valet and a glutton, and was often employed by Harlequin. The relationship between Pierrot and Harlequin is the prototype followed by Sancho Panza and Don Quixote, and by Gogo and Didi.[13]

In many respects Harlequin resembles Don Quixote. Harlequin is occasionally given to philosophy, has trouble distinguishing reality from illusion, dwells in a fantasy world, and has "a weakness for inventing a distinguished parentage for himself."[14] Didi and Don Quixote are the most imaginative adaptations of Harlequin to appear in their respective ages.[15] For such reasons critics have noted similarities between this comic tradition and Beckett's. Deeper bonds of affinity may also be observed from attentive comparison of Cervantes's and Beckett's main characters.[16]

One of the traits that Beckett and Cervantes share is an acute sensitivity to character names. Functions are revealed through appellation. Just as there has been a good deal of speculation on the origins of the names Didi and Gogo, much has been written about the possible origins of Sancho.[17] The character's most outstanding feature is indicated by his name,

Sancho Panza, which means Saintly Paunch or Holy Belly. Onomastically this gastronomical allusion indicates the usual inclination of his habits. Sancho eats and sustains the life forces, whereas his master prefers abstinence in order to maintain his high level of consciousness in a realm beyond everyday reality. Sometimes the servant is known as Sancho Zancas, a title referring to his legs, thus suggesting his attachment to the earth.

Beckett's sensitivity to such a naming process is shown in *Endgame,* for example, where the two main characters are called Hamm and Clov. In much the same manner he gives a culinary designation to Didi's companion, Estragon (in English, Tarragon). Like Sancho, Estragon appears at first to be inferior in intelligence to his friend. He consumes scraps of food thrown away by passersby, constantly mispronounces names, is not quite certain about his friend's mission, yet remains more or less faithful, and, thanks to Vladimir's interference between him and Lucky, he is the victim of undeserved beatings. Didi's partner also bears a double designation and is sometimes known as Gogo. His principal name, Estragon, designates an herb that reputedly contains properties capable of curing his companion's unnamed genitourinary malady. Gastronomically and etymologically, Gogo's main appellation provides additional clues to his identity and function. According to the *Encyclopédie Larousse,* "L'estragon est employé comme stimulant, apéritif et stomachique." Consider also W. W. Skeat's view of this term's derivation: "Thus the strange form *tarragon* is nothing but *dragon* in a form changed by passing through an Oriental language, and decked in Spanish with a Latin suffix (viz. − tia)."[18] Gogo can be considered a demonic counterpart to Didi, a monster responsible for his companion's downfall. The maleficent character of Sancho and Gogo will be treated in greater detail below.

Despite their differences, both sets of buffoons form complementary interdependent pairs. Just as the subordinate characters' names are fraught with suggestiveness, the names of the pairs' superior members are equally rich in associations. The etymological roots of Don Quixote's various names give clues to his character and have a bearing on our understanding of Beckett's play. Scholars cannot exactly agree on Cervantes's original intention in choosing various names for the Knight of the Sad Countenance: he is also known as Quixada, Quesada, Quixotiz, and finally Alonso Quixano. Since the novel is supposed to be a parody of chivalric literature, the evidence tends to support the belief that the name Quixote was patterned after the knight-errant Lanzarote, insofar as the gentleman from La Mancha selects his own name after an illustrious predecessor. Cervantes, moreover, could have chosen this name, as Leo Spitzer suggests, because it sounds like a hybrid term incorporating "quij-," meaning jaw, with the humorous suffix "-ote," producing in effect the implication that here is a foolish man who is addicted to words, language, ideals, and philosophy.[19] The jaw is the organ of loquacity and this disposition is reflected in the name. Another widely shared suggestion concerning this name (one not entertained by Spitzer, however) is that it could be derived from a special term designating a piece of armor used in covering the thigh.[20]

   In all these literary associations it is important to keep in mind the advice of the critic Constantino Comneno, who states that such eponymic identifications should be taken "not in a literal but in a metaphorical sense."[21] After all, Cervantes does devote much attention to the knight's armor and to his weakness for words. His selection of that particular piece of armor to be included in a name may have Freudian overtones, hinting at the hero's extreme vulnerability in his quest for ultimate beauty and salvation.

   From a similar linguistic perspective it is possible to conjecture that Beckett selects the designation Godot in order to suggest the elusive, multiple nature of his central character. As with the fools' names, there is room for various associations to be established. Ruby Cohn points out that although the equation of Godot with God may be too simplistic, the name does seem to be for most readers some sort of composite title suggesting a union of the deity with a pejorative ending.[22] The suffix "-ot" in French bears the same comic resonance as "-ote" in Spanish with, however, a slightly more denigrating overtone. The connection of Godot, who never seems to appear, with the other characters will become clearer below.

In her analysis of the vagabonds' nicknames Cohn also states that Didi and Gogo reflect their primary functions, namely telling (French, *dire*) and going (English, *to go*). In fact *gogo* is simply colloquial French for a naïve being, a booby; thus Gogo's name and function resemble those of Sancho, who fulfills the equivalent Spanish theatrical role of the *bobo,* thus reflecting the same type of character.

Vladimir, who usually answers to Didi, bears a Slavic saint's name meaning "ruler of the world." He also answers to Mister Albert, "illustrious through nobility." He may be reluctant to remain with his companion, for his Slavic name might suggest some sort of Latin-Teutonic barbarism implying "fly with me." But like Harlequin and Pierrot, and like Don Quixote and Sancho Panza, these two form a complementary comic pair whose only certainty is that they are condemned to remain together in a quest they scarcely understand.

Vladimir is neatly though not completely differentiated from Estragon during the initial discussion of their ailments. The latter clearly complains about his foot problems, whereas the former, painfully shuffling about "with short, stiff strides, legs wide apart" (p.7), seems to suffer from some obscure malady of the pubic region. It may simply be some sort of urinary trouble afflicting the kidneys, of the same

type which plagued Don Quixote. Or it may be an attack
of the clap to which Beckett refers in the play. In the case
of Vladimir it will be shown below how his name may reflect this painful illness.

It is a commonplace of criticism to reduce Sancho and
Don Quixote to an allegorical pair of antithetical, irrecon-
cilable attitudes: the real as opposed to the ideal, the materialistic in conflict with the spiritual. Much the same has been
written about the relationship between Estragon and Vladimir.
These are obvious oversimplifications. Upon closer scrutiny
their relationship is one of interchangeability and its complexity is borne out in the unfolding of their adventures
and in comparing their names to those of the other couple
in Beckett's play.

Now that the names of these characters have been investigated, some attention can be paid to how they function in
similar circumstances. Cervantes's work is as rich in detail
as Beckett's is apparently sparse. Indeed, one critical view
of Beckett's world is that nothing happens. It may seem
overly ambitious to try to compare the 126 chapters of
the novel with the 2 acts of the play. Yet it is possible to
avoid doing violence to the texts of either classic, to focus
on certain episodes of similar concern which are similar in
detail and design and which reinforce the conclusions derived
from examining the protagonists' names.

Beckett's play is structured around a series of dialogues,
and Cervantes's novel, according to the Hispanic scholar,
Francisco Márquez Villanueva, can also be viewed as orga-
nized by this principle.[23] Certain common minor details seem
similar, such as Sancho's and Gogo's uneasiness about eating
turnips and their understanding of the fate of hanged thieves,
but these are probably coincidental and bear no intrinsic relationship to one another. Other episodes, however, are worth
considering because they tend to confirm common themes
that are basic to both works.

Don Quixote's confusion of the mundane and the marvelous is a well-known facet of the character. He mistakes a barber's basin for Mambrino's helmet, refuses to be dissuaded, and insists on wearing it, hoping to gain, somehow, from the magical powers he believes it will confer upon him (pt.1, chap. 21). His vision of this simple headgear allows him to enter into his fantasy world with more boldness and justification. Sancho does not really understand his master's enthusiasm, but he joins in the game by stripping the barber's mule for his own profit. Sancho also suffers from what Spitzer terms "polyonomasia," a tendency to confuse words.[24] And so does Estragon, particularly in his encounter with Pozzo, which will be examined below in greater detail.

This defect in language, however, serves more than comic purposes; it allows the reader to penetrate the various levels of linguistic and psychological perspectives offered by the author. In this instance Sancho refers to Mambrino's helmet as belonging to "Malino," the Evil One. He senses the strange, numinous power it possesses, at least in his master's imagination. In this connection it should be noted that the headgear of Pozzo's servant, Lucky, also seems endowed with special powers. On two occasions Lucky's hat is supposed to permit its wearer to enter into higher spiritual realms. In act 1 Lucky wears it while delivering his famous monologue, and in act 2 Vladimir tries it on during his imitation of Lucky's role, although on this occasion he is not compelled to utter a similar tirade. In both works the hat seems empowered to stimulate the imagination, to allow the wearer to enter another dimension of perception. Lucky cannot "think" without his headgear.

There are other episodes in the novel and play which point to a kindred spirit. At the outset of his adventures Don Quixote comes upon a young shepherd named Andrés, who is being beaten by his master for having lost some sheep. One is reminded here of the young messenger who announces

Godot's nonarrivals, and upon questioning, he reveals that
Godot beats his brother who, like Andrés, minds sheep. Both
Sancho and Estragon are victims of mysterious and inexplica-
ble thrashings which their companions strive to avert. Regarding violence and misplaced charity, Sancho and his master
come upon a group of galley slaves whom they promptly
set free, and as a reward for their compassion they are abused
and stoned by their thankless beneficiaries (pt.1, chap. 22).
This episode brings to mind Estragon's initial concern for
Lucky the slave who then kicks him in the leg for his effort
to help. In the two instances solicitude for brutes goes unap-
preciated.

In the second part of Cervantes's work, master and squire
undergo one of the most bizarre experiences in the novel,
the descent into the cave of Montesinos (pt. 2, chap. 22).
No scene more clearly illustrates the gap separating their
perceptions of reality. Although he spent a single hour in
the hole according to Sancho, the knight insisted that he
was there for at least three days and three nights, and that
he had finally beheld the vision of his beloved Dulcinea del
Toboso. Sancho indulges his master's fancies but sardonically
muses that when he himself fell into a hole he saw no beauti-
ful vision but only toads and snakes (pt. 2, chap. 55). No
episode more openly underscores the incompatibility of
the pair's views and the native intelligence of the unsophis-
ticated subordinate in conflict with his superior.

Estragon and Vladimir react in a similar manner to the
arrivals of Pozzo, whose name means "well" or "hole" in
Italian and suggests a creature of infernal origins. Some
critics see in Pozzo the true identity of Godot because he
seems to arrive just when the latter is expected. The question
is not quite as simple as this, but if Pozzo is the Godot whom
Vladimir awaits, he would indeed be as monstrous as Aldonza
Lorenzo (Don Quixote's pure Dulcinea) is vulgar. On three
occasions Estragon identifies Pozzo as the awaited one. And

upon arrival the idealist of the pair, Vladimir, cannot admit reality. Though the circumstantial details differ, the encounters underlie the visionary's reluctance, protected by some mysterious shield, to surrender to common sense, to abandon his noble vision in spite of the evidence. While these incidental details of novel and play are similar, there are other bonds of affinity equally convincing which confirm the relationships between the two sets of companions.

Throughout the novel and play one is struck by the attention the authors devote to encounters with passersby. Though Don Quixote meets a much greater number and variety of strangers than Estragon and Vladimir do, it is possible to narrow the focus to one significant type of meeting: the encounter with the self. It is through the medium of apparently chance meetings that the elusive truth may be sought, that the encounter with various aspects of the self may be realized. The denial of the knight's imaginative powers is not directly achieved by the good intentions of his friends to bring him back to reality; he has seen the other side and he likes it. Rather, his enchantment is affected indirectly when the knight recognizes, quite by accident it would seem, that his true nature, the reflection of himself, is seen in other characters.

The most revealing episode of this type is the account of the wild man called Cardenio and his madness. Sancho and his master discuss the strange hermit, and for a moment Don Quixote appears to be on the verge of recognizing his own madness, but he quickly lapses into his autistic illusions. Cardenio's manner of speaking is similar to that of Lucky, the slave of Pozzo. He too speaks rapidly, frenetically, without any interruptions. Just as Cardenio is supposed to mark Don Quixote's first encounter with himself, so Lucky holds up a mirror to Vladimir. The lessons pass unobserved by the interested parties.

The importance of these meetings of kindred individuals

is heightened by the encounters with Sansón Carrasco. The bachelor has been sent twice by fellow townspeople to beat the knight at his own game in order to induce him to return home and to sanity. At first Carrasco appears as the Knight of the Mirrors and then as the Knight of the White Moon. His contrived titles indicate his function of a mirror to reflect the truth to the beholder. Between these two chapters there is another revealing encounter, this time with Diego de Miranda, the Knight of the Green Coat, the prototype of the reasonable human being, the man of Aristotelian moderation and supine mediocrity (pt. 2, chaps. 16 and 18). His name is also doubly meaningful. Miranda is simply the present participle derived from the verb *admirarse,* which is the most frequently used word by Cervantes in the novel, a term which literally means "to look at oneself."[25] This name crops up again at the beginning of Lucky's speech and serves, among other functions, as a speculum to project back the image of the self. In the case of Cervantes, Diego's title may indicate the mythical origins of his role as a healer of lunatics.[26]

So much for the secondary episodic similarities in the works of Beckett and Cervantes. On a deeper level we also find similarities in their handling of the problems relating to self-knowledge and identity.[27] It is important to note that both authors employ the artifice of the play-within-a-play in order to reinforce and give depth to that central notion of their works, the complex relationship of reality and illusion. Cervantes uses the device on several occasions, as with Master Pedro's puppet show and with the actors from the traveling company representing the courts of death, for example. These miniature plays staged to shock the knight to his senses are rich in detail and extremely varied. But they all lead up to the central profound and subtle development in the novel which has been sensitively treated by Salvador de Madariaga: Sancho and Don Quixote gradually,

almost imperceptibly, exchange roles.[28] The decline of the
master and the rise of the servant should not, however, be
interpreted as the triumph of realism over idealism. On the
contrary, Sancho only manages to succeed his master at the
cost of becoming more like Don Quixote himself.

In Beckett's case Estragon and Vladimir engage in a brief
play-within-the-play during the second act in which they too
exchange roles. Here they imitate Lucky and Pozzo, playing
those roles which correspond to their relations in the natu-
ralistic frame of the drama. The sharp division between
their allegorical roles pitting reality against illusion is there-
by reduced, and, as Ruby Cohn remarks, the distinctions
separating Beckett's tramps tend to blur until there is a
fusion of sorts between personality and character.[29] This
type of personality joining is often obscured, however, when
the play-within-the-play is neglected as a reflecting device
capable of dramatically conveying a great theatrical and
psychological truth. When Gogo and Didi put on the skit
and assume the roles of Pozzo and Lucky they are in effect
indirectly telling themselves and us that their relationship
of leader and follower is better reflected in the relations
between master and slave as seen in the other couple.

This radical transformation is not effected without a
certain degree of violence and dislocation toward each character.[30] In one instance, to underscore the antagonism between master and servant, Sancho turns on Don Quixote
and beats him out of exasperation (pt. 2, chap. 60). As
Madariaga observes: "Sancho is, up to a point, a transposition of Don Quixote in a different key."[31] Not only are
the squire and master personifications of opposing forces;
they also incarnate on another level a subtle fusion of these
same forces when they exchange roles with one another.

This transformation is equally subtle in Beckett's play.
After the little play in the second act, Estragon strikes Lucky
and Vladimir hits Pozzo. They are striking each other through

the characters whose parts they have just taken in the play-within-the-play. The master and slave here are transpositions of the tramps, and their brutal relationship is but a contrapuntal magnification, a grotesque exaggeration of Vladimir's and Estragon's relationship. Just as Vladimir promises Estragon salvation by Godot's arrival, Pozzo (who always arrives when the latter is expected) leads Lucky off to the market of the Holy Savior. Pozzo's actions are a burlesque, a vengeful mockery, of Vladimir's. Vladimir must convince the carnal Estragon that his spiritual vision will prevail. The intellectual fears the brute; thus he feels obliged to perpetuate the illusion of Godot's advent in order to keep Estragon from realizing that their true relationship is better reflected in the grotesque pair of clowns represented by Pozzo and Lucky. The violence attending this metamorphosis should not be construed as merely the subordinate's revenge. The reason for it is more complex than this. The role transfer is the only means by which the process of *desengaño* — "undeception" — can be effected.

The similarities among character names emphasize this psychological and dramatic tension. The sad clowns of Cervantes and Beckett do their best to avoid the confrontation with the self or at least with the realization of the absence of the self. Despite their friendships they cannot really go on together. Don Quixote, once returned to sanity, has no choice but to die. It should be emphasized that the novel's end is not as grim as it appears. The knight does not vanish completely, for his spirit is carried on by the squire. Though he is moving in the same direction by the end of the play, Vladimir, too, manages to forestall the disintegration of his spirit.

Indeed the main thrust of Beckett's work is that these opposing forces are fatefully, not fatally, linked. Vladimir and Estragon suffer from what David Grossvogel calls "the difficulty of dying." Like Don Quixote they would like to put an end to it all, but they cannot; they are forced, like the sinners in Dante's *Inferno* and Sartre's *Huis Clos,* to resign themselves to eternal torment.

Beckett's characters are not entirely disenchanted. They may have some vague glimmer into their true condition, but the principle of hope, though shaken, is not completely shattered. If for no other reason it must be preserved as a defense against utter nihilism. Especially in Vladimir's case it seems to persist in his illusory expectation. It is the only excuse at hand for going on. Without this he would despair and die. But he does not. In the end Vladimir appears to continue in the same old manner. Now he may no longer believe with complete assurance; he may not even believe any longer in his mission; but he persists, though with the doubt in mind that his task has lost some of its former certainty.

Vladimir's suffering may be endless, but he is not without some modest sign of awareness. Throughout the absurd vigil he is told that Godot's arrival will be postponed till tomorrow.[32] After meeting Pozzo and Lucky for the first and then the second time, his faith is somewhat shaken, an uneasiness to which he cryptically alludes: "Now it's all over. It's already to-morrow" (p. 50). Vladimir may realize here that his expectation is ill-founded, that his ideal vision of Godot will never materialize, for the simple reason that his real image is already present in his fellow man. By this discrete dramatic transposition of perspective, exemplified by the reversed mirror image of the plays-within-the-play, Don Quixote and Vladimir are almost defeated by the brutal weight of reality represented in the projected grotesque apparitions of their spiritual subordinates. The spirit rarely survives such encounters. Reality threatens to triumph in the end and allow the spirit to linger on as a token of its charming, indefatigable impotence.[33]

The figure of the clown is well suited to maintain this fine distinction between tragedy and comedy. Only his words and his names allow him to carry on. Cervantes and Beckett have derived their onomastic techniques and their main characters from the Italian comic tradition and have adapted them to their own dramatic purposes.[34] The barren landscape of La Mancha is similar to Beckett's wastelands where life is barely sustained. Beckett's embodiment of the intellect may bear a stronger resemblance to Kierkegaard's knight of the infinite resignation than to Cervantes's Knight of the Sad Countenance. Still, Sancho Panza probably loves his master and Estragon may remain with his partner, *faute de mieux*. But their associations must ultimately prove to be precarious and perilous.

Cervantes and Beckett stand at opposite poles of Western civilization but the axis remains the same. Beckett, of course, stands much closer to our own time; thus his treatment of the sad clowns seems to have been colored as well by similar efforts carried out during his own life span. But the influence of the Italian comic tradition is long and varied. David Madden observes, "Commedia influenced Goldoni, Lope de Vega, and Shakespeare, and, through silent slapstick, its verve and its more profound implications are seen in Beckett's *Waiting for Godot*."[35] Since Beckett chose to present his versions of commedia types in shapes more related to his times, it would be profitable to examine them in the light of those authors who exerted the greatest influence over the development of his imagination. After Cervantes, Shakespeare and especially Joyce, through their handling of the play-within-a-play device and their onomastic inventiveness, were helpful to Beckett in his treatment of character growth.

3. Transfiguration

We walk through ourselves, meeting robbers, ghosts,
giants, old men, young men, wives, widows, brothers-
in-love. But always meeting ourselves.

JAMES JOYCE

Didi and Gogo, though descendants of Don Quixote and
Sancho Panza, are also rooted in the twentieth century.
The play appears to take place nowhere in particular, but
the clowns' costumes and concerns suggest a modern setting. Didi and Gogo exchange roles as their earlier Spanish
counterparts do, but Beckett has articulated their specific
anguish with an eye to the present — not just that eternal
present that he is fond of evoking, but the present of his
own generation. Their plight is reflected and amplified by
the associations conjured up by their names. The various
appellations given to Lucky are no less significant and their
examination will constitute the main focus of this chapter.

In order to appreciate Lucky's role, brief mention should
be made in passing of two literary techniques used by Beckett
— the psychological double and the play-within-a-play. They
will help elucidate some of the play's enigmatic linguistic features. More important, consideration of these themes will reinforce the significance of naming characters and will help us
understand the sources, among them particularly James Joyce,
from whom Beckett derived his onomastic techniques.

With reference to the dramatic theme Renée Riese Hubert
states that "the plays within the play that he [Beckett] constantly and consciously stages assume great dimensions."[1]

Unfortunately these dimensions are not indicated. In this
chapter I shall discuss, with emphasis on the influence of
James Joyce, various possibilities which should put these
key dramatic elements, particularly plays-within-plays, into
perspective and relate them to Beckett's handling of character growth and naming.

To begin with, all Beckett's works, in English and in French,
have been aptly described by critic Katharine Worth as "those
shadow twins."[2] The overall atmosphere of *Waiting for Godot*
is suffused with an eerie duality: it is divided into two acts,
Vladimir and Estragon possess two sets of names, and with
Pozzo and Lucky, there are two couples. Godot's promised
arrival is twice heralded, apparently by two different boys,
and the master and slave show up twice on stage. Freud once
remarked that whenever two humans make love there are
really four people in the room. The same sort of analogy
by way of *dédoublement* could be extended to Beckett's
characters. Didi and Gogo are bound together by certain
ties of affection and are frequently annoyed by their mutual
lack of appreciation regarding their respective doubts. These
differences in temperament do not prevent them from con-
templating, however vaguely, the underlying stresses of their
relationship. This is the primary reason for Beckett's introducing Pozzo and Lucky to the tramps. The playwright is
presenting the tramps with a dramatic magnification of their
own relationship. Pozzo and Lucky are the doubles of Gogo
and Didi. Their connection with the tramps is on the order
of the *Doppelgänger*, and close analysis of their names will
demonstrate how Beckett reinforces this association. In this
chapter it will be shown how Beckett follows and departs
from Joyce's naming techniques and how character names
are employed by both authors to present the *dédoublement*
of personality.[3]

Like Joyce, Beckett transforms his art and transfigures his
characters through use of the double.[4] In order to solve the

dramatic problem of relating the roles of the two tramps to those of the master and slave, of depicting them as doubles, Beckett employs two theatrical techniques: the dumb show and the play-within-a-play. In the second part of *Waiting for Godot* the author joins these two contrivances in much the same way that Shakespeare did in the second part of *Hamlet*.[5]

Onomastic techniques are mainly literary devices. Beckett strengthens them through recourse to these two dramatic artifices in order to show how each of the tramps, but particularly Didi, avoids confrontation with the double. It is important to notice that the shock of recognition is delayed until the climax of the drama, and even here it is doubtful whether Didi actually manages to see clearly. This is the reason Beckett has Gogo perform a dumb show with Didi and then has both take part in a play-within-the-play. The purpose of these performances is to imitate Pozzo and Lucky, and, more significantly, to link the two couples, to present them as doubles in order to stress the monodramatic quality of the play. The two tramps never quite seem to arrive consciously at this horrendous moment of truth, the cognizance of identity, of self-knowledge. What they are lacking is indirectly suggested through their names and is unconsciously experienced through the latent manifestation of the double as expressed in the brief pantomime and skit that they stage toward the middle of the second act of the piece.

There exists at once an essential kinship and an estrangement between Didi and Gogo. Like Sancho Panza, Gogo is the link between his master and the real world. Against his better judgment and instinctive wisdom Gogo grudgingly remains with his idealistic friend. Each time Gogo wishes to leave, Didi reminds him, often in vaguely religious terms, of their common mission, of their obligation to remain steadfast in their vigil and to keep faith.

Their fidelity to self-ignorance is contrapuntally accentuated by their stage business which occasionally gropes toward self-knowledge. The brief double performance that the two companions engage in during the second act is initiated by pratfalls and hat tricks borrowed from the stock routines of the music hall, circus, and silent films of comedy. Most critics have tended to gloss over this rapidly executed exchange of hats. But this game they play, ostensibly to help them pass the time, is related to the general structure of the work and to the short skit in which they assume the roles of Lucky and Pozzo.[6] What these buffoons perform is more than a mere Laurel and Hardy routine. Beckett surely had the style of these film clowns in mind when he wrote the passage, but as is so often the case with him the scene has deeper reverberations.

On the stage the hat exchange routine dazzles the audience and seems to pass too quickly. In the text it only appears as stage directions that are all too easy to gloss over. While it is significant that Didi ends up with Lucky's hat on his head and that it does not trigger any flow of words similar to Lucky's famous speech, it should be noticed that this hat passes successively between them. Didi thus appears to exchange roles with Gogo, who plays Pozzo's part, and Gogo, too, has a chance to wear the slave's hat, to enter briefly into his part. In these two minuscule performances Beckett is trying to convey two basic impressions. First the clowns' roles are in a constant state of flux and exchange, and secondly the clowns' counterparts are to be found in the other couple. Here Beckett's use of diversion and play as means to come to grips with reality must not be underestimated.[7] Beckett's choice in using nonverbal language before words also reflects his debt to the Neapolitan philosopher Giambattista Vico, for whom the basis of language was to be found in prelingual gesture. Didi and Gogo are in effect saying what cannot be said. In this crucial scene their roles have been reversed thus exposing, however briefly, their underlying interdependence in which the spirit no longer controls matter and Didi is no longer the dominant partner in the couple.

Games and play are invoked here to express the inexpress-

ible, to allude indirectly to truths too horrific to be confronted openly. On the literary level it will be shown that the
character names perform the same function as these games.
This similarity of functions is at the heart of Freud's notions
about humor, with special reference to the technique of
punning which he regarded to be the lowest form of the
verbal joke.[8] Thus nonverbal language as gesture and verbal
expression as punning stand close together in the play. The
transition from one realm to another reinforces the suspi-
cion that the play's multiple dimensions are in close relationship and harmony. The very baseness of the pun is of particular interest for the reader of Beckett's play because punning, along with the figure of the literary double, has been
transformed and transfigured by the playwright's alchemy
in the second act of the piece into a high symbolic mode
of revelation. The two techniques converge to reveal the
characters' identities and functions. In *Murphy* Beckett
writes: "In the beginning was the pun." Wordplay and stage
games are combined to add a new dimension to the significance of the second act and to the drama as a whole.

With reference to the comic routine of rapid hat exchanges,
it has been stressed that this interplay is not just a diversion;
it is closely related to the preceding episode in the first act
where Lucky delivers his insane speech in rapid fashion. The
quick execution of the hat exchanges could be thought of
as a parallel to speedy pronunciation of all the characters'
names. The assonantal similarity of the couples' names should
provide Didi with a clue to their relationship, but the intuition eludes him. This is probably the reason why Beckett
gives the tramps two sets of names. Their dual identity was
meant to remain elusive.

This ignorance on Didi's part reflects the central theme of
nonrecognition of reality in the play.[9] Vladimir is especially
incapable of perceiving the deficiencies of his expectations
and the identity of Godot. Estragon, though less sophisticat-

ed in appearance, unconsciously goes to the heart of the matter when he thinks he sees Godot in Pozzo and tries to accord him that name. Three times he identifies the slave master as the awaited one, and on each occasion he is rebuked by Vladimir, who by the third time, however, begins to waver ever so slightly in his blind faith. But Estragon may be closer to the truth regarding identities. His intuition and the tramps' common desire to assume momentarily the roles of Pozzo and Lucky lift for a brief moment the veil of self-deception. The short mime which they perform also serves another function. Writing about Cervantes's masterpiece, Marthe Robert, for example, observes: "Like those insects who protect themselves against their nearest and strongest enemies by a mimetic ruse, quixotism apes the manner, tone, and gestures of its anonymous adversary."[10] The same could be said of Beckett's tramps who are reluctant to tackle Godot head on. Estragon's bumbling attempt to assign him a name reflects the dual purpose of Beckett's use of language: it simultaneously reveals and protects the bearer of the name.

At this point attention paid to the importance of the names will be useful in understanding the confrontation. As noted above, puns and vivid stage business assume a major part in Beckett's dramas. The exchange of roles on the part of his couples has already been noted, for example, in *Endgame*. The range of suggestiveness evoked by the characters' names in that play seems considerable, and a good case has been made for linking, nominally, the pair Hamm and Clov with Nag and Nell.

In *Endgame* the secondary characters could be considered to be the parents of Hamm, and as such they reflect on a different level the same conflict operating between Hamm and Clov. It has been observed that the name Clov might suggest the French word for "nail" and link him to Nag (German "Nagel" for nail) just as Hamm, who endlessly torments the younger Clov, suggests the instruments of persecution (in the form of a hammer). On the more playful level of punning perhaps these names, Hamm and Clov, have culinary associations as well. What is important to observe in these confrontations is the clash not just between the generations but throughout the generations, three in this case.

The suggestive richness of the tramps' formal names has been examined in the first chapter of this study. And various interpretations have been put forward to explain Vladimir's and Estragon's nicknames. Simply enough, Didi is a French term of endearment and Gogo is used of a simpleton. To one critic these names bring to mind, respectively, French and English babytalk for the word God. In Beckett's dramaturgy there are no definite, static interpretations. The names are deliberately ambiguous in order to provoke responses on different levels. No one explanation is possible because Beckett always prefers to keep the scene in motion. But it should be made clear that these nicknames are phonetically linked to the characters whom the tramps are mimicking in their playlet. When Didi plays Lucky and Gogo plays Pozzo, the hidden architecture of *Waiting for Godot* shifts on its axis. The music hall surface is that of dream and nightmare, and the dreamer is Beckett's audience and actors alike, who witness the changing events of the dream through the character mutations of Didi and Gogo.

The subtle transfiguration of these characters is not seen through their stage business alone; it is also perceived in psychological and philosophical dimensions which have some bearing on the functions of their names. Psychologically, Beckett's actors can rarely tell the difference between reality and illusion. They never actually attain that fullness of self-knowledge which is the hallmark of classical tragedy. It is for this reason that Beckett chose to add the designation *tragicomedy* to his English version of the play. He thrusts the inquiry deeper than the casual encounter of tramps and passersby, trying to elicit from actor and audience a sophisticated response to the confrontation with unacceptable reality. In the midst of this confusion, which marks the final meeting of the two couples, it is important to remember that Vladimir acknowledges, resignedly, their common identity with the only other mortals who appear to inhabit their lonely universe: "All mankind is us, whether we like it or not" (p. 51).

When Vladimir confronts Lucky and Pozzo for the second time, there is still no startling reversal or rejection of their stage relationship, no direct intuitive recognition on his part that the one he awaits never arrives, that their world is emptier, more lonely than he had thought possible: "Yes, in this immense confusion one thing alone is clear. We are waiting for Godot to come" (p. 51). Not much seems to have changed during the two acts. However, Vladimir may be approaching the truth — that his image of Godot will never manifest itself and that the endless expectation is but a pretext to continue and prolong what comedians call the game of life. This resignation is not excessively stoical but it is a reflective position that bears responsibility for the speculative atmosphere which engulfs this play.

On the philosophical level Alain Robbe-Grillet's essay on *Waiting for Godot* begins with a useful inventory of various interpretations of the identities attributed to Godot, all of which he rejects in favor of his own.[11] Briefly, the novelist-critic declares that the two vagabonds are really waiting for themselves, that there is no need for appeals to external factors or to intricate symbolism to explain their vigil. Throughout this essay, however, Robbe-Grillet relies heavily upon Heideggerian and Sartrean concepts to reinforce his view that the continuous presence of Didi and Gogo on the stage, in the world, is the unique constant condition, the sufficient proof of their *Dasein* or their "being there" to justify the central function of their existence. Throughout his works Beckett has not been reticent about his employment of symbolic systems to enrich his creations. And although the philosophical viewpoint may be useful, the same vision may be gleaned from the text itself, without necessary recourse to external speculative structures. The words are closer to the mark, and Beckett's use of the play-within-the-play more apposite, than the philosophical influences that have been thought to be at work upon the playwright. His play is never made but always in the making; its open-ended structure does not allow completion or one single interpretation to predominate.

It has been necessary to examine the dramatic, philosophical, and psychological features of the play in order to understand the literary sources Beckett draws upon to express character transfiguration. Whatever the extent to which Beckett is indebted to formal speculative systems for his portrayal of the self's pilgrimage, his greatest debt is without doubt to his own imagination and appreciation of literature. Beckett surely owes a great deal to James Joyce's vision of individual and multiple transformations of his characters' personalities through onomastic manipulation. Throughout the various stages of the eternal recurrence found in the works of both authors, the words of Joyce hold fast: "The soul of everyelsesbody rolled into its olesoleself." Despite their fundamental differences, Joyce and Beckett both strive to produce the effect of a unity of opposites by means of a sophisticated handling of circumlocutions primarily through comedy, irony, and parody and only secondarily through philosophy. It is beyond the scope of this study to review every aspect of their association. Emphasis will be devoted and limited to onomastic techniques and the themes conveyed by this device. Both Beckett and Joyce are masters at punning and devising fantastic character names to give flesh to their respective creativity. As Martin Esslin observes: "Beckett is as fond as Joyce of subtle and recondite literary allusions."[12]

Beckett seems to owe a great deal to Joyce in the matter

of Lucky's name. Naming devices as such rarely stand independent of other literary considerations. They are often employed to emphasize various themes. In order to appreciate Beckett and to identify the link between him and Joyce an examination of related points is essential. The association of these two artists surely constitutes one of the more important literary relationships of this century. Because rather little has been written on this topic, an examination of their similar literary intentions is in order insofar as it bears upon the complex development of the naming process. On the question of Joyce's influence on Beckett regarding onomastics, a basic paradox must always be borne in mind: through his own fantastic character names, Joyce believed he was achieving a total integration of language. Beckett was initially drawn to a similar strain of creativeness but in the unfolding of his long career it becomes apparent that he is aiming at the disintegration of language. This is the importance of *Waiting for Godot* in the focus of this study. As we have seen, the piece stands midway in Beckett's career and contains elements derived from his early years and elements that point to his more recent works. What is exceptional about this play is that its language has apparently been pared down without loss of its rich suggestiveness.

Critics have not found it easy to determine the exact nature of the relationship between Beckett and Joyce. The few details known lead one to conclude that theirs was a fruitful, creative association in spite of the inevitable frictions that develop between two literary geniuses. It is acknowledged that Beckett was a close witness and confidant in the creative unfolding of Joyce's final masterpiece. Joyce used to read him passages from his work in progress. Beckett returned this kindness by praising and explicating his mentor's work in the 1929 essay, "Dante ... Bruno . Vico . . Joyce." There have been but few treatments of their relationship, and one of the more curious of these was put forward by Lionel Abel.

In his study on the theater Abel asserts that Pozzo and Lucky
as well as Hamm and Clov reflect the master-slave relationship
that he claims existed between the two Irish writers living in
Paris. Abel feels that Hamm, blind and preoccupied with his
work in progress, fits the image of Joyce toward the end of
his association with Beckett.[13]

At first glance this interpretation appears irrelevant, and it
is undoubtedly impertinent, for there is no evidence to support this dismal view of their collaboration. The influence of
Joyce upon Beckett was not sadistic but linguistic. However,
although one does not find any serious allusion to the relationship in Beckett's works, one can, while rereading *Finnegans
Wake,* occasionally stumble across cryptic phrases in the
shape of names which have been thought to refer to Beckett.
Adaline Glasheen, in her glossary of characters in the *Wake,*
identifies the name "Bethicket" with Beckett.[14] And there
may be other echoes of their friendship: one also reads: "He
was. Sordid Sam, a dour decent deblancer, the unwashed,
haunted always by his ham."[15] Toward the end of the *Wake*
one finds: "Sam knows bettern me how to work the mira-
cle" (p. 467).[16] Although Joyce is more or less referring to
himself here, to his connection with the "beurlads scoel,"
the line has an eerie prophetic air about it insofar as Beckett
through his major works seems to have captured a larger
audience with equally complex and closely related ideas.
What is remarkable is that Beckett's handling of names is
just as rich as Joyce's although it has not yet attracted as
much critical commentary. If these references somehow
point to Beckett it demonstrates that even on a personal
level name-punning is observable in their friendship and art.

The influence of Joyce on Beckett, particularly through
Finnegans Wake, cannot be easily overlooked. Even so,
comparison of Joyce's luxuriant masterpiece, festooned in
overwrought digressions, with Beckett's simple dramatic
frame may at first seem misplaced in some degree. Joyce's

very active world bears scant external resemblance to Beckett's, where nothing is supposed to happen. Stylistically, Joyce's language is elaborate, labyrinthine, and convoluted — in short, all that Beckett's seems not to be. But from bits and snatches of conversation and the general architecture of *Finnegans Wake* certain common features do stand out, details related to the play-within-a-play artifice, the transformation of character, and onomastic devices.

The most poignant common theme that readily comes to mind is the transmigration of the self, the transfiguration of the individual through a series of increasingly complex circumstances. In an original study on this topic, G. C. Barnard traces the theme of schizophrenia through all Beckett's novels and plays.[17] Although the approach provides fresh insight, the study sometimes leaves the impression that Beckett's work constitutes a dramatic casebook on mental disorders. But Beckett is not a psychologist per se, although psychological themes can be discerned in his creations. He is above all an artist who prefers to deal with ideas related but always subordinated to these fields of inquiry. Barnard, too, admits that Beckett is preeminently an artist. But if the playwright's work suggests some views on God and the development of the self, then these notions would be more appropriately discussed within the perspective of Beckett's aesthetic experiences and treatment of the subject. His association with Joyce should shed some light on this handling of character naming and development.

Finnegans Wake is without doubt the most elaborate and ambitious literary attempt to reflect the transfigurations of the self through name changes. By means of a myriad of plays-within-plays the same characters keep dreamily encountering themselves in multiple disguises. These reveries evolve into a fantastic meditation on the various roles assumed by the twin sons, Kevin and Jerry, of the protagonist, H. C. Earwicker. Uncertainty is the hallmark of Joyce's and Beckett's major

works. It is no more clear what Earwicker's crime was than
it is certain that Godot will really come.

Throughout the vicissitudes of their multiple adventures
and identity changes, two persistent themes stand out: the
eternal confrontation between the artist and the philistine,
the victim and persecutor, and their interchangeable roles.
This relationship is pertinent for understanding the roles
and names of Pozzo and Lucky. We have already seen that
Joyce was a reader of Vico and was interested in his view
of history. Joyce also made use of another thinker, Giordano
Bruno, from whom he borrowed the doctrine of identified
contraries. Aspects of both of these philosophies were treated
by Beckett in his first essay on Joyce.[18] This dramatic combination of philosophies provides the principal impetus for
Joyce's work, and it is intriguing to consider that its complexity was not lost on Beckett as he pursued his own quest for
creating personality changes. Looking at these books of Joyce
and Beckett it gradually becomes apparent that on the whole
the cyclical movement of time returns upon itself in order to
simulate a sense of progression at the heart of an ever-recurring
universe where the past and present seem to melt into the
future. This temporal scheme may also be observed in Beckett's
play. And its unfolding is parallel to the pattern of constantly
shifting name changes.

The crimes of Joyce's Earwicker and Beckett's tramps are
never made entirely clear, but what they have done may simply be linked to the ontological crime of existing, of being
alive. Neither Joyce nor Beckett views the existential pain
of living from the tragic angle of an Aeschylus, for example.
For them it is set in a contemporary frame despite references
to archaic symbols. In Joyce despair is expressed by a "dummp-
show" in which one brother complains how hard it is "to
mpe mporn." Although this curious spelling is supposed to
suggest Greek, it is neither Ancient nor New Testament Greek:
Joyce has transliterated Modern Greek spelling to intimate

the question of existence in a contemporary post-Christian setting. Recourse to this particular atmosphere is also evident in Beckett's choice of name for Pozzo's slave.

In *Waiting for Godot* Beckett casts this lament in the words of Estragon as "our being born" (p. 8). Immediately following the lament he begins to muse: "I remember the maps of the Holy Land. Coloured they were. Very pretty. The Dead Sea was pale blue. The very look of it made me thirsty. That's where we'll go, I used to say, that's where we'll go for our honeymoon. We'll swim. We'll be happy" (p. 8). A honeymoon with whom? Surely not with Vladimir. Their union would be barren, sterile, bereft of life — not much unlike their present existence. Thus one suspects that they are already in the Holy Land, that their future is already unfolding itself in the present. In *Ulysses* Joyce, with reference to the same locale, takes somewhat longer to convey an identical dual meaning. When Bloom visits the porkbutcher's shop, for example, he observes the butcher wrapping up some sausages in a sheet of newspaper on which is printed an idyllic description of the new Zionist settlements in what was then a barren corner of the Ottoman Empire. Two pages later Bloom is musing over the citrus fruit shipped all the way from Jaffa and suddenly his vision of the New Jerusalem begins to cloud over: "A dead sea in a dead land, grey and old. Old now. It bore the oldest, the first race. A bent hag crossed from Cassidy's clutching a noggin bottle by the neck. The oldest people. Wandered far away over the earth, captivity to captivity, multiplying, dying, being born everywhere. It lay there now now. Now it could bear no more. Dead: an old woman's: the grey sunken cunt of the world" (p. 73). Here Bloom, the Everyman of vaguely Jewish origins, contemplates the significance of his forebears' ancestral homeland. This same conflict in identity is reflected in Estragon when he puzzles over the question of Lucky's hat. It should be recalled that in the original manuscript version of the play Estragon's

name was Lévy. In both novel and play the images of life and
death coexist simultaneously with reference to the promised
land. Didi and Gogo seem to function like twins, alternately
pondering their chances for salvation and crucifixion. But in
this play the true order of twinning takes place between members of the different couples: Didi is more closely related to
Lucky through assonance and circumstance. His overt conflict may be with Gogo but his covert struggle tends toward
Lucky and the latter's subordination to the gross taskmaster
called Pozzo.

To illustrate the eternal conflict between twins Joyce employs ingenious onomastic manipulations in the *Wake*. He
first casts them as the primitive clowns Mutt and Jute, names
inspired by the comic figures of Mutt and Jeff. Jute is sitting
before a cave entrance drinking from a skull and "seemeth a
dragon man." The designation applies equally to his fierce bearing and to his role as a dragoman, a Middle Eastern term sig-
nifying a servant or traveling companion. This episode is mentioned only because it immediately follows the allusion to
Beckett as "Bethicket" in the *Wake*. Some of these opening
passages of the *Wake*, when carefully examined, reflect in part
the naming devices and religious symbolism later developed
by Beckett for his own purposes.

Intimations of Beckett's play may perhaps be perceived
in this section of the novel. In the confusion of speech the
question is asked: "Who ails tongue coddeau, aspace of dumb-
illsilly? And they fell upong one another: and themselves
they have fallen" (p. 15). William York Tindall deciphers
the first part of this phrase thus: "Où est ton cadeau, espèce
d'imbécile?"[19] What is uncanny here is that even in its English form one may dimly perceive Godot's name standing
out. And the second part of this quotation brings to mind
the climax of *Waiting for Godot* when all the characters
collapse together on the stage and seem to blend their sep-

arate identities for a brief moment. It is a minor point, but the wordplay is reminiscent of the overall comic atmosphere and general purpose achieved by both artists. And in the spirit of stage tricks Mutt and Jute then "swop hats" like Didi and Gogo in order to make themselves indistinguishable. In a later metamorphosis the brothers reappear as a "music-hall pair." This aspect of low-comedy stage representation is sustained by various references to the dimeshow, the dump-show, thumbshow, and finally a dumb show which is preced-ed by a description of their parents' bedroom wall where there hangs a picture of Saint Michael, armed and slaying Satan and the dragon. Didi and Gogo put on their own dumb show and arm themselves against a demonic enemy whose presence is as elusive as it is terrifying.

Still resorting to wordplay and conforming to the music hall atmosphere, Joyce reintroduces the fraternal conflict in a "boudeville song" in which the opposing theological systems of Docetism and what he calls "Didicism" are weighed. Here one may perhaps perceive another source for Vladimir's nickname. Before remarking on the function of Didicism, mention must briefly be made of Docetism, the earliest of all heresies, which held that Christ's carnal body was not real and therefore was incapable of suffering. Docetism was in part a precursor of that series of heterodox beliefs such as Christian Gnosticism and Manichaeism which were based on a radical dualism governing the universe and a fundamental antithesis between matter and spirit. More than just an affirmation of the evil nature of matter, Doce-tism first posed the philosophical question of appearances to Christianity. The most famous Docetist was Marcion, whose doctrine and influence on Joyce and Beckett will be examined below. There are intimations of these ancient be-liefs in Beckett's play, especially when the two tramps, strug-gling with Gogo's boot, begin to evoke the idea of appearances:

Estragon: We always find something, eh Didi, to give us the impression
we exist?
Vladimir: (impatiently). Yes, yes, we're magicians, But let us persevere
in what we have resolved, before we forget. (p. 44)

It should also be mentioned in passing that the legendary
founder of Docetism was Simon Magus the sorcerer and
magician. The recurrent theme of the defective memory
afflicts everyone in Beckett's play. In the second act Gogo
scarcely recognizes Pozzo and Lucky, who in turn do not
remember meeting Gogo and Didi the day before. And Didi
is not sure of the day when Godot is supposed to arrive. More
than merely underlining the uncertainty of existence, these
memory lapses serve to throw into question the very possibility of recognition and knowledge of reality.

So much for Docetism, which was a real chapter in the
history of theology. But what about Didicism? Joyce coined
this word to suggest a viewpoint contrary to Docetism in
which real suffering is reaffirmed. This is the perspective
upheld by Didi; thus it is reasonable to assume that Beckett
had this term in mind when he came to give a name to this
character.

It is also possible that Didi's name was partly inspired by
the last contributor to *Our Exagmination* who called himself
Vladimir Dixon. According to Sylvia Beach in her 1961 introduction to this volume, Stuart Gilbert suspected that this
person was none other than Joyce himself. Perhaps, too,
one of the origins of the name Didi is classical. Referring
to the ancient Celtic priests, Lucan writes in his *Pharsalia:*
"Vobis auctoribus umbrae/non tacitas Erebi sedes Ditisque
profundi/pallida regna petunt." "And it is you who say
that the shades of the dead seek not the silent land of Erebus
and the pale halls of Pluto." And continuing, "Rather, you
tell us that the same spirit has a body again elsewhere, and
that death, if what you sing is true, is but the midpoint of
long life." Julius Caesar commented that the Druids believed

that Celts were descended from Dis Pater, the Roman counterpart of Pluto, the god of the dead. *Did* is a contraction
of *Ditis* and like the Greek *ploutos* it signifies "rich." This
might suggest Beckett's obsession with death in the connection between Didi and Pozzo. Regarding this last derivation
of the name, an observation by Vivian Mercier is especially
apt: "Indeed, Pozzo's blindness reminds me that Plutus, the
Greek god of earth, was always represented as blind."[20]

The antagonism between the concepts of Docetism and
Didicism finds echoes in Gogo's and Didi's early conversation
about the reality of their entire range of aches and pains
which neither is able to grasp sympathetically. The moment
when Didi admits that they are magicians is set in the context of Gogo's struggle with his boots. Gogo suffers through
his feet and Didi through his head. In the first act Gogo's
boots are too tight but in the second act another larger pair
has miraculously appeared. Didi tries to explain that someone else must have switched pairs, an explanation that fails
to satisfy his companion.

This exasperating exchange of opinions probably harks
back to the earlier conversation dealing with the Gospel
story of the two thieves where Vladimir says: "There's man
all over for you, blaming on his boots the faults of his feet"
(p. 8). In the French version Vladimir says here: "C'est son
pied le coupable," which is a pun referring to the *coups de
pied* that Estragon gives and receives, and it implies that his
suffering is in large measure self-inflicted and equivocal. Here
Beckett contemplates the memorable words of Saint Augustine:
"Do not despair: one of the thieves was saved; do not pre-
sume: one of the thieves was damned."[21]

Beckett and Joyce both use elaborate puns in character
names in order to reflect the theme of cosmic and personal
ambivalence. Both devote attention to the respective fates
of the two thieves who were crucified next to Christ. It is
from this setting that Beckett probably derives the name

for Lucky. In the hands of these artists the names of the
thieves are no less revealing of the roles they play than is
their source in the Third Gospel. Joyce indicated that his
meditation on the thieves' crucifixion was also to be found
in another holy text. He liked to compare the architecture
of *Finnegans Wake* to the labyrinthine art of the Book of
Kells, the most elaborate example of ancient Celtic manuscript illumination. Joyce is chiefly interested in the "tene-
brous *Tunc* page" on which is written in glorious illumination:
"Tunc crucifixerunt XPI cum eo duos latrones." Although
this particular page is from the Gospel of Matthew, Joyce
insinuates that its origin, in his use of the legend, may be
better expressed in Luke, the same Gospel to which Beckett
indirectly refers in identical circumstances.

It may be of interest to note in passing that Joyce's discussion of the Book of Kells occurs on that page containing the
already quoted oblique reference to Beckett and the sin of
human existence. With regard to the latter, Didi's mention
of "our being born" is immediately followed by his reflection upon the Gospel variations relating to the two thieves.
Beckett has already referred to this famous biblical paradox
in other works. In *Murphy* the character Neary encourages
others to go on because one thief was redeemed, and in
Mercier et Camier, considered to be the precursor of *Waiting
for Godot*, the two tramps liken themselves to the crucified
thieves. In *Godot* Didi argues that despite narrative incongru-
ities among the four Gospels, "it's a reasonable percentage"
that one of the thieves was saved. Beckett clearly had in mind
Luke, and to French ears the name of Pozzo's slave suggests
this evangelist. Lucky is tormented by a diabolical master,
and the fact that the Latin version of the slave's name is
Faustus indicates another line of investigation which is too
complicated to be pursued here.

Like Beckett, Joyce was intrigued by the possibilities of
puns on the name of the third evangelist. In his treatment

of the thieves' narrative Joyce has ambitious designs. He
begins with a parody of Sir Edward Sullivan's study of the
Book of Kells, using it as a springboard for introducing another central theme of his work, the Manifesto of Anna Livia
Plurabelle, the mysterious "Mamafesta" of the earth goddess,
"Anna the Allmaziful." Though this enigmatic letter origi-
nates from Boston, the adventures recounted in the text
probably took place in Lucalizod, a compound word com-
bining two Dublin suburbs, Lucan and Chapelizod. Joyce
often reintroduces the four evangelists in various guises,
but it is Luke whose name is most frequently repeated
throughout the text, in which he turns up as Lucas, Lucan,
Laird of Lucanhof, Lukky, and perhaps as Lucky the artist
to be sold "dirt cheap at a sovereign a skull" (p. 374). Of all
the Joycean transfigurations of the third evangelist this last
reference comes closest to fitting the description of Pozzo's
slave.

The comparison between Joyce's Luke and Beckett's Lucky
should not be forced. To be consistent with the animal symbolism of the Gospel tradition Beckett would probably have
referred to Lucky as a calf, the usual graphic sign of Luke.
Pozzo instead always calls Lucky a pig, a swine. But then
one recalls that Joyce, too, refers to "the ninethest pork
of a man . . . Lucky Swayne" and "he luked upon the bloom-
ingrund where ongly his corns were growning" (pp. 223 and
326).[22] It is worth noting that Lucky's name may be derived
from Lucifer. Pozzo refers to him as formerly "my good
angel." Perhaps the name also stems in part from Lucia
Joyce, the daughter of James Joyce. She loved Beckett
and later on she ended up in a state of insanity, a condition which is often said to afflict Lucky.

The references to Luke occur in the most complicated
part of the *Wake,* and the associated themes cannot and
need not all be listed here. For Joyce they mainly point
to the trials of Shem the Penman, the artist persecuted by

the philistines. For Joyce and Beckett the Third Gospel was the most promising area in holy writ to borrow from. Here the prominence accorded to the Third Person of the Trinity suggested a religious setting in which to explore the relationships and manifestations of the Holy Ghost. This theme of messianic expectation and transfiguration is accorded a central place in the works of Joyce and Beckett. It is linked to the trials of the suffering servant at the hands of the master.

The relationship of Lucky and Pozzo is anticipated in many passages of the *Wake*. Joyce, like Beckett, is concerned with the interrelatedness of character types and names. It is Joyce's intention to conceive various sets of circumstances in which the soul of the artist would evolve. One of the most elaborate offerings is in the form of a parody of La Fontaine's tale based on Aesop's fable of the grasshopper and the ant. In Joyce's hands this story is elaborately developed but its analysis is warranted here simply because it prefigures much that occurs between Pozzo and Lucky. Beckett's treatment of the relationship of master and slave has its immediate source in Joyce's handling of the conflict between artist and philistine.

Simply stated in the original Aesopian version, the ant refuses to aid the grasshopper who sang all summer, and condemns her to dance all winter. Joyce's most detailed and ambitious treatment of this encounter is in the story of the Ondt and the Gracehoper, and as might be expected their names indicate their roles. Ondt is the Danish word for evil and an anagram of Don't.[23]

In order to project more effectively the horrific presence of this dominating lord, Joyce reintroduces him in various guises. This depiction was not lost on Beckett, who uses it to present Pozzo as the tormentor of Lucky. As the embodiment of the materialistic, prosaic persecutor, the master is destined to torment the poet who seeks (or used to seek) grace through art. But as if to exemplify Bruno's law of merging opposites the two characters tend to blur together. Ultimately they will complete the progressive unfolding of the Trinity: "Three in one, one in three. Shem and Shaun and the shame that sunders em" (p. 526). Before this final stage is reached in Joyce's work the two brothers must remain antagonists and they are chiefly remembered for this conflict. They need each other, for even their spiritual discrepancies are complementary and their union would symbolize dramatically the completion of psychological reconciliation. Ideally this merging is supposed to produce a combination of the disparate cosmic forces at play, but there is just as good a chance that the result may in fact produce a monster more terrifying than previously witnessed in their separate identities. Their mutual dependency and conflict are similar to the connection between Pozzo and Lucky, and their names reveal their fate.

It is somewhat easier to compare Didi and Gogo as a complementary couple than Pozzo and Lucky. The former appear related in dress and activity whereas the latter typify the clash between master and slave. But upon closer observation there are equally strong bonds on an onomastic level that suggest that this pair too is destined to be together. Vladimir cannot understand why Pozzo treats Lucky so brutally, why their relationship exists at all. Pozzo answers: "Remark that I might have just as well been in his shoes and he in mine. If chance had not willed otherwise" (p. 21). This confession and reference to fate resembles the previous discussion about the two thieves and the one's salvation and the other's damnation. All of Pozzo's bearing and actions call to mind an irritated deity. When Vladimir does inquire about Lucky's mistreatment, he retorts: "A moment ago you were calling me Sir, in fear and trembling. Now you're asking me questions. No good will come of this!" (p. 20). The tramps still fail to understand why the master keeps the slave who obviously displeases him so much. Pozzo does not reply directly but says: "As though

I were short of slaves!" In the fifth part of *Textes pour Rien*
written in 1950, about one year after the play, there appears
the solitary question: "Why did Pozzo leave home? He had
a castle and servants."[24]

This remark is reminiscent of the first question usually
suggested in a child's catechism, the question concerning
the purpose behind God's creation of man. If God is omnip-
otent and omniscient why did he feel the need to create
so miserable a creature as the human being? The orthodox
response postulates the wish of God to share the glory of
creation with someone else, to have someone to love him
in return for his generosity.

Beckett's use of character names is not exclusively con-
fined to biblical sources. Classical mythology is also invoked.
Immediately after this remark about slaves Pozzo refers to
Lucky as "Atlas, son of Jupiter." This is a purposely misleading statement. Atlas is not the son of Jupiter but of Iapetus
(Japhet, O.T.?). In this mingling of names one can detect a
fusion of the Viconian ordering of time, the transition from
the divine to the heroic. Moreover, the distant strains of
cosmic discord are also felt. Iapetus, father of Atlas and
Prometheus, was considered to be the ancestor of humanity
by the Greeks; he was also reported to have been cast into
Tartarus for rebelling against Zeus. These disparate elements
and legends do converge in the encounter of Atlas and
Hercules when the Titan tricks the hero into supporting
the heavens. But there are other references to Greek mythology in this play which are worth noting and have bearing on
the naming process.

Just after Didi returns from one of his periodic trips offstage apparently to relieve himself, Pozzo resumes the series
of histrionic displays which he has been performing for their
benefit. All the characters need audiences for their role-
playing and they go to great lengths to remind the theater
audience that what is being performed on stage is precisely

a play. Their frequent asides directed to the gallery interrupt any conventional theatrical illusions. Pozzo dramatically calls: "Listen! Pan sleeps" (p. 24). It is impossible to tell whether this is merely a gratuitous interjection or another mythological reference to his slave who is always on the verge of collapsing or falling asleep. In mythology Pan is represented as half-man, half-goat, and Gogo thinks the dance that Lucky now performs might be called "the Scapegoat's Agony." In the French version proof of the interchangeability of roles is more elaborately expressed.

Here Didi identifies this dance as "la mort du lampiste." This term is onomastically relevant. The *lampiste,* literally the lamplighter, signifies in popular French a flunky who is forced to bear the responsibilities of his superiors. The word also designates the person in the theater who is charged with keeping small receptacles called "godets" and "lampions" filled with combustible materials and wicks. A few pages before this reference to Lucky's dance achievements, when Pozzo mentions Pan, Pozzo confusedly refers to the tramps' appointment "with a Godin ... Godet ... Godot" (p. 24). As in the torture of the Gracehoper at the hands of the Ondt, Lucky, the former artist, is the whipping boy of Pozzo, and in both cases allusions to fire suggest the chief means of this torment.

When Pozzo utters the phrase "Pan sleeps," he no doubt intends to evoke the legend of Pan's irascible temperament, the image of the forest god who did not like to be disturbed during his midday rest. He reputedly had a terrifying voice, possessed prophetic powers, and fell in love with the nymph Echo. As a god of the forest, Pan also suffered. It is said that when Arcadian hunters were disappointed in the chase, they scourged his statue in order to beat new life into the divinity who supposedly reigned over them and the forest. The father of Pan is Hermes, like the son an Arcadian, a demon who occupies a stone pile by the roadside for magical effects.[25]

The Greek Hermes became associated with the Egyptian god of art, Thoth, and as such was known as Hermes Trismegistus. Joyce identified himself closely with the thrice great Hermes as the perfect divine symbol worthy of the artist's calling and respect. Lucky's career partly conforms to these legendary descriptions. Lucky, when disturbed by a well-intentioned Gogo, kicks him in the shins and Pozzo must resort to beatings in order to force him to perform his arts for the benefit of the two vagabonds. In the painful process of self-discovery through a series of short skits and playlets, Didi and Gogo initially are not even aware of the direction their requests tend to lead them. Gogo with his stinking feet cannot move on and Didi with his stinking breath cannot reason. They ask Pozzo to make Lucky perform the tasks that they are themselves incapable of mastering.

The clearest onomastic indication, albeit incomplete, of Lucky's role is brought out only in the French version. Here Pozzo calls his servant a "knouk" and adds in the English version that "formerly one had buffoons. Now one has knooks." It is obvious that the strange word, found in no dictionary in either of its forms, has been coined by Beckett and has something to do with fools and jesters. The implication is that clowns have been replaced by a new type of fool more in keeping with modern times. Some critics think they have found the source of this term in the Russian word "knout" or whip. But this word does not have the same ending as the English term. However, this may be of little importance because the term invented by Beckett belongs to a type of wide imaginative range; it is a highly sophisticated portmanteau word which is supposed to evoke several meanings at the same time.

Joyce raised this low-comedy device to a high level, and all his character names bear multiple significances. Perhaps Beckett, in considering the slave's name, was entertaining a particular reference frequently used by Joyce throughout the *Wake*. According to A. Walton Litz's study of that book, Joyce's Earwicker is compared with a hero from a seventeenth-century novel by Aphra Behn, *Oroonoko; or, The Royal Slave*. This certainly fits Lucky's status and the last part of this name resembles that of his calling. The first part, *oro*, states Litz, is a Latin verb meaning "to speak," thus "Oroonoko" may be paraphrased as "the talking clown."[26]

Perhaps the word "knouk," or "knook" in the English version, may also be attributed to more immediate experiences and personal observations from Beckett's early years in Ireland. It is recorded that Beckett was born on Good Friday, 13 April 1906, in a suburb of Dublin called Foxrock. A young man of his sensitivity for language could not fail to be impressed by the rich suggestiveness of Irish and Celtic place-names. In the vicinity of Foxrock one discovers towns called Kilgobbin, Leopardstown with its Stillorgan Castle converted into an asylum, the village of Stillorgan itself, Bushy Park, Golden Ball, Galloping Green Stepaside, and Dundrum. Beckett's memory may have been drawn at times to the region just northwest of Dublin, an area to which Joyce frequently alluded in his novels. Perhaps this was the original locale of Pozzo's castle with its many servants.

In all likelihood Beckett's strange neologism for a clown had its origins in this area and is derived from anglicized forms of Celtic words. In northwest Dublin, upon leaving Phoenix Park — where Earwicker's crime supposedly took place — one can pass by Mount Joy, then push through the Knockmaroon Gate toward Chapelizod and Lucan with its Swift Hospital for the insane. Or one can set forth through the Castleknock Gate, past the great clock tower toward Knockmaroon Hill, whose summit is occupied by the village of Castleknock called in Gaelic "Caesla Cnucha." This spot is important in Irish mythology, for here Comhal, the father of Finn, the great hero, was killed in battle. The Irish word for hill is *cnuc* and this is an exact phonetic replication of

the term knook. The Gaelic *cnucha,* sometimes spelled *cnoc,*
is transcribed into English as "knock" and in this form, while
retaining its original pronunciation, Lucky's role and function
may be revealed. Beckett's imaginative inventiveness and use
of such place-names may seem strange to non-Gaelic readers,
but various critics have confirmed similar verbal play in
his poetry.

In its anglicized form "knock" also suggests a low German
cognate *knuk,* and knocks are what Lucky receives from
Pozzo and Gogo.[27] Related to the Teutonic derivations,
the term also evokes an aspect of the imitative word "knack"
which according to one of Joyce's favorite sourcebooks,
Skeat's *Etymological Dictionary,* signifies "a jester's trick,
piece of dexterity." According to the *Oxford English Dictionary* a "knacker" is "one who sings in a lively manner," which
might suggest Pozzo's recollection of Lucky's early calling as
an entertainer and instructor. This same dictionary also re-
cords that the term refers to a "trickster, deceiver," and on
a more ominous level, keeping in mind Lucky's infamous
speech, the word indicates "one who buys old houses, ships
etc., for the sake of their materials, or what can be made of
them." (In his speech Lucky, it will be remembered, spews
forth odd bits and pieces of philosophy and literature.) In
British dialect "knacker" used to refer to "an old worn-out
horse" thus suggesting Lucky's bestial appearance and beast-
ly treatment.

Lucky's curious title given by Pozzo was intended to be
polyvalent. Once again a Gaelic usage may hold the key to
the slave's most important task. In the Scottish dialect a clock
is known as a "knock," and the most revealing part of Lucky's
famous three-page monologue deals mainly with the problem
of time. Pozzo, the master of space, cannot tolerate Lucky
and claims that the slave, like Didi and Gogo, is tormenting
him with the notion of time. Perhaps Lucky is also Pozzo's
timepiece, attached to him as if by a watch chain and carry-

ing a suitcase full of sand. The theme of time in Beckett's
work has been exhaustively treated by other critics from
the philosophical point of view. The image of Lucky as a
timepiece, a mechanical man gone berserk, tends to reinforce this theme, along with the artist's choice of symbols
and word repetition.

Careful examination of the wordplay in Lucky's speech
reveals the sources of Beckett's inspiration. The fantastic
monologue is set, literally and figuratively, in Joyce country.
By this, however, it is not implied that Beckett offers here
a parody of Joyce's art. It is safe to assume that he has no
intention of ridiculing the art of his mentor. Neither does
he employ a slavish imitation of Joyce's techniques despite
some apparent encouragement from this source. For the
most part Beckett adapts Joycean techniques of wordplay
and delivery to his dramatic needs in order to serve his own
vision of reality.

In this central scene Lucky is forced to think by Pozzo
as a consequence of Didi's wish to see him perform. Request
and performance reinforce the onomastic link between the
assonant names. Lucky's speech is as memorable as the tramps'
pantomime is easy to overlook. However both performances
are plays-within-the-play, inserted to emphasize a complex
scheme of things for actors and audience. The slave's outburst is the dramatic high point of the piece; all other wordplay pales in comparison with this torrential hemorrhage of
knowledge streaming from the lips of Lucky. And when heard
onstage the slave's tirade is, superficially, a mockery of human
vanity attempting to impose order on chaos. The monologue
consists of bits and scraps of undigested information and
misinformation, the detritus of old school-notes and theological treatises. Yet from beneath the apparent gibberish
of Lucky's speech a certain pattern of associations emerges
in the course of a careful reading. Lucky's soliloquy seems
at first to be entirely improvisatory in organization, but it

possesses an underlying structure that is revealed by examination of individual words.

Lucky's first utterances are the stock phrases from innumerable third-rate philosophical treatises, the "works of Puncher and Wattman of a personal God quaquaquaqua without white beard . . . outside time" (p. 28). This opening sentence suggests two phrases of Joyce's invention from the *Wake:* "Wachtman . . . punkt by his curserbog" (p. 556) and "He lifts the lifewand and the dumb speak — quoiquoiquoiquoiquoiquoiquoi!" (p. 195). The first phrase is taken from the passage that describes the trial of Earwicker. To say that he is "punkt by his curserbog" may mean in a sort of German that he is on time by his *Kursbuch* or train schedule. But since these are Joycean portmanteau words, they have other associations as well. "Curserbog" could stand for "damned (or damning) God" from the Slavic "Bog," meaning God. Thus the watchman or time man could have been punched by a cursed God, which is similar to what Lucky says at the beginning of his speech and to what he endures throughout the play at the hands of Pozzo. Lucky visibly occupies the subordinate role in this couple. But if Pozzo is to be believed, the roles of tormentor and tormented can be exchanged.

The second phrase cited above is used by Joyce to introduce the Anna Livia narrative and is uttered by Shem in the shape of Mercius the artist who in his misery has only the artist's gift of words to redeem and express himself. Joyce uses the French form *quoi* (*what*) whereas Beckett employs for double effect the Latin *qua* (*as*) which has the same sound as *quoi* in French. In both cases the artist comes to life exclaiming wonderment and confusion.

The very next words pronounced by Lucky in his speech consist of a series of nouns, "apathia, athambia, and aphasia," all modified by "divine." Divine apathy clearly refers to the imperviousness, even indifference, of God toward human endeavors and entreaties. As such this term is close in meaning to what Jung has referred to as "euphoric apathy" or *la*

belle indifférence, usually in connection with hysterical manifestations but here mainly in reference to the gods. Intimately
related to apathy is divine *athambia* which signifies imper-
turbability. This term is the negative of the Greek *thambos*
meaning amazement. But why such a confusion of tongues?
Clearly Beckett wills it so, for the third word of the series,
aphasia, is a speech disorder associated with schizophrenia.
Strictly speaking, Lucky's use of language is more akin to
a subcategory of aphasia — paraphrasia: he tends to say
the same thing repeatedly in other words.

In his psychological study of the play, G. C. Barnard
also notes this neurotic dysfunction of normal speech
patterns in Lucky's monologue. And he also recognizes
"the combination of two mutually contradictory ideas,"
such as God's love and God's indifference, paradoxes given
wild expression by Lucky.[28] Verbally, Beckett emphasizes
the frustrating inability to explain divine providence or
simply to account for its contradictory twists. In the *Wake*
Joyce is reflecting this same concern as mirrored down
through history. With both artists duplicity of language
is called upon to simulate this basic uncertainty in the
cosmic order.

In Lucky's speech the sense of wonder has been both
denied and affirmed. If divine athambia stands for the negation of amazement, the fourth term in the series of heaven-
ly attributes, the divine Miranda, stands for its affirmation.
Miranda is another key word for understanding Lucky's
speech. As has already been noted, this term shares func-
tional and nominal affinities with Don Diego de Miranda
in *Don Quixote* and perhaps with that minor character in
the *Wake,* Lieutenant Buckley of H.M.S. *Miranda.* In any
event they all derive as names ultimately from the Latin
mirandus which signifies that which calls forth wonder
and amazement, the basic reaction to be aroused by
philosophy according to Aristotle.

As a name, Miranda is linked to the Latin *miror* and ultimately to English *mirror*, and thus serves as a reflection or reflective device for the self. And it surely must refer to the heroine of *The Tempest*, "for reasons unknown but time will tell and suffers like the divine Miranda."[29] That Beckett undoubtedly has Shakespeare uppermost in mind here is borne out by three subtle allusions. Time is specifically mentioned in three places in the speech by Lucky and perhaps alluded to on four occasions in the form of the sports term "tennis." In these references to such gratuitous activities as football, running, cycling, swimming, flying, and so forth, tennis constantly reappears. Lucky's mind is bouncing back and forth like a tennis ball between the courts of reason and madness. The word tennis, in connection with Miranda, may be a mumbled pronunciation of *Tempest* or even *tempus,* and certainly it is used to evoke a sense of the multiple effects of time. Early in the *Tempest* Miranda says: "Oh I have suffered with those that I saw suffer." The effect of Lucky's speech is not just to dazzle the audience and to dismay the other actors; it was meant to draw them together, to help them see the cohesive link between the madman and the three actors accompanying him, and to emphasize their common suffering, plight, and identity.

On a philosophical and dramatic level Lucky's role is clearly related to the notion of time. Quite literally, this preoccupation with temporality is reinforced by Beckett's development of ambivalent terms and language play. In contradistinction to the mentioning of Shakespeare's play and God in this tirade, Beckett employs low-comedy elements to mock the philosophers in scatological language: "the Acacacacademy of Anthropopopometry of Essy-in-Possy of Testew and Cunard." Cunard here may refer to Nancy Cunard who, with Richard Aldington, awarded a prize to Beckett for his first published poem, "Whoroscope," which was later printed by her at the Hours Press. In the French version of the play Cunard is replaced by Conard, the name of the Paris publishing house noted for its scholarly editions of literary classics. At the other end of the spectrum the scatological suggestiveness of Cunard and Conard is easy to detect since it is uttered along with the lines "in view of the labours of Fartov and Belcher." Commenting on this speech, G. C. Barnard finds the words "Feckham Peckham Fulham Clapham" quite out of context.[30] But a careful rereading of these curious names shows that they may have something to do with Didi's speculation about Pozzo's relationship to a family whose "mother had the clap." The entire speech exudes decadence and decomposition "in spite of the strides of alimentation and defecation wastes and pine wastes" (p. 29). This reflects Gogo's search for food and Didi's frequent trips offstage. While the obscene meanings are obvious, it is not easy to tell whether these words are personal names or place-names. Perhaps in the back of Beckett's memory there was a recollection of that Irish writer called Charles Kickham (the author of *Knocknagow*), mentioned by Joyce in his work. Certainly these strange words somehow refer to those three outlying districts of London — Peckham, Fulham, and Clapham. What is certain is that allusions to venereal disease and "penicilline and succedanea" again state the case for the even odds in the central struggle between decomposition and damnation and the possible alternative of salvation.

The substitution of the philosopher Berkeley for Voltaire in the English version might be viewed as a concession to a different audience's ear. But Samuel Barclay Beckett's fascination with his fellow Irishman and alumnus of Dublin's Trinity College has already been noted by others. What particularly enchanted Beckett was Berkeley's famous notion about perception. His dictum *esse est percipi* — to be is to be perceived — stands as the device for Beckett's characters who struggle mightily to discern and ignore their surroundings and the double images of themselves.

Another significant change in the second version of the
play is the substitution of Normandie for Connemara. Associations of all sorts arise here. In Lucky's gibberish Connemara
could suggest anything from Gomorrah and gonorrhea to
connerie and even Golgotha, especially considering the skull
mentioned at the end of his speech. Here Beckett mentions
"good round figures stark naked in the stockinged feet in
Connemara." This may be a prophetic vision of Gogo to
whom in the second act Didi says: "Perhaps you'll have
socks some day" (p. 29). Such predictions are not borne
out, for at the very end of the play instead of Gogo's get-
ting his socks, his trousers fall down.

There are other elements in Lucky's diatribe which justify
regarding the term "knouk" as suggestive of a timepiece. In
the last part of the speech two dominant images are intro-
duced, stones and a skull, which reflect, respectively, time-
lessness and the transitory nature of all things. Progressing
from the labors of Fartov and Belcher, Lucky then goes on
to the works of Steinweg and Peterman, that is to say, stone-
way and stoneman. Connemara, situated on the savage west
coast of Ireland on Galway Bay, is noted as a stone-strewn
wilderness. It is pure speculation but Connemara might hold
some personal memory for Beckett inasmuch as the family
of James Joyce came from there, a fact in which Joyce took
great pride, according to Richard Ellmann. Connemara is
also known as Joyce country after the famous clan which
bears that name, so it is not surprising that this region should
hold special fondness for Joyce and that it was remembered
by Beckett.

Why Beckett chose this particular area of Ireland to mention must of course remain conjectural, like much else in his
works. The theme of temporality is once again suggested by
Lucky's chief philosophical function. Perhaps Beckett recalled
a reference from *Ulysses:* "a timepiece of striated Connemara marble stopped" (p. 831). When one remembers that

Lucky seems to act like a timepiece that gradually petrifies and comes to a halt, this analogy is not so farfetched.[31] Lucky suggests the spirit of time and thought just as Pozzo seems to be the master of space and matter. Thus this speech begun by Lucky is not only a mockery of thinking; it is this and more. It is the pitiful attempt of the spirit to assert its domain against the forces that conspire to crush it. Not as noble as Pascal's thinking reed, rather more on the order of Dostoevsky's Kirillov perhaps, but nonetheless a spirit to be reckoned with.

Lucky's verbal hemorrhage is the linguistic tour de force of the play. The end of his outburst, with its references to the skull, may serve to link the tramps' wait by the tree and their fear of death with Christ's suffering on Golgotha. The transformation of Beckett's barren tree into one that bears a few leaves parallels the biblical myths of the tree of knowledge and the tree or cross of salvation as they appear respectively in Eden and at Golgotha. Lucky's mention of the skull and stones reminds the tramps of their eternal vigil, recurring attempts at suicide, and endless crucifixion upon Calvary in the shape of mutual, uncomprehending antagonism. In time and throughout time they are forced to remain and wait for a Messiah who will not come because he is already there. Through manipulation of language and names Beckett gives multiple dimensions to their vigil. William Tindall observes this same pattern of contrasting images as the basis for the successive metamorphoses of Earwicker's son: "The first of many recurrent conflicts between ear and eye or time and space or stick and stone (Shem as ear-time-tree and Shaun as eye-space-stone) this conflict comes like all the rest, to nothing."[32] In *Finnegans Wake* there are no clear boundaries between the characters' successive transformations. And so it is with Beckett's clowns, forever condemned to tolerate an eternal wait for promised salvation and probable disappointment.

It is customary in contrasting these two writers to set

Joyce's abundance against Beckett's leanness, to treat Joyce more or less as the optimist and Beckett as the pessimist. In the broadest effects of their works this may be the sense conveyed. Joyce, for all his *tristitia,* seems to reaffirm the forces of life and creativity in contradistinction to the pervading air of doom that has been attributed to Beckett's works. Joyce was spiritually a member of a select generation of post-Symbolist writers who still believed in the supremacy of art as the refuge against nihilism. Through his depiction of accumulated human experiences Joyce tends to emphasize space, whereas Beckett through his Spartan decor stresses the realm of time. In order to compensate for his major play's apparent leanness Beckett relies in great measure on names to convey the mutability of his protagonists.

Temporality occupies a central position in the works of both artists. Their fascination with the effects of time is indicated through their treatment of certain common religious traditions and character names. While the Viconian time scheme was the obvious philosophical frame of the *Wake,* there is another complementary system of temporal dimensions underlying its architecture, a religious vision of time to which Joyce occasionally refers and to which Beckett is also indebted. Joyce was intrigued, indeed haunted, by the idea of the hypostatic union of God and man in Christ. His spiritual guide, according to William Tindall, was Hermes-Thoth, the patron of writers and legendary founder of the esoteric tradition.[33] Beckett, too, was influenced by this tradition and its implications have a direct bearing on the way the playwright came to fashion his characters' names.

Joyce brooded over the implicit assumptions of the dogma of the Trinity. For him the thought of the Second Coming was fraught with wonder and dread, the same kind of awe that possessed Beckett's characters during the long vigil. The most radical interpreter of the Trinity was Joachim de Floris, the medieval Calabrian monk and mystic whose works,

which Joyce read in the "stagnant bay" of March's library
in Dublin, are mentioned in *Ulysses* and perhaps in the *Wake*
as Florian's fables. According to Joachim, the god which supposedly emerged in the New Testament is actually opposed
to the god of the Old Testament, and ultimately the deity
will undergo another metamorphosis in the guise of the Holy
Ghost. In such a radical ground plan of biblical exegesis Joyce
found a congenial reciprocity of opposites that allowed him
to develop the myriad transformations of the self.

Beckett makes no direct reference to the Joachimite tradition, but in view of his long association with his mentor it
seems unlikely that he was not familiar with its basic outlines. *Waiting for Godot* may also be viewed from this perspective as a play cast in the form of the Joachimite prophecy.[34] In both works art and the unfolding of the self
in time and through time take precedence over theology
and philosophy, which have been pressed into the service
of the artist. If Beckett was influenced by this particular
tradition it was not because of mere antiquarian curiosity.
Concern for the implications of the Trinitarian dogma is
intimately related to the theme of character change and
transformation as reflected in the metamorphosis of various names.

In sum, the brief play-within-the-play staged by Didi and
Gogo points the way to Lucky and Pozzo as grotesque cari-
catures of the two tramps, distorted images of themselves
forever locked in the vise of illusion and ignorance. The
master-and-slave couple is not presented for contrast with
the vagabond couple: Pozzo and Lucky reflect the roles of
Gogo and Didi with the parts reversed and transmogrified,
with spirit now at the mercy of matter. This literary device,
the play-within-the-play, is primarily aimed at the representation of multidimensional truths, and it attempts to make a
balanced appeal to the audience's sympathy, to enable it to
appreciate better the complex dramatic and psychological

conflicts set within a parody of a religious framework. Just as with the characters created by Joyce, the demands of self-knowledge are too awful to be confronted directly. Beckett's handling of names and themes associated with onomastic devices remains the major vehicle capable of permitting some degree of revelation. Now that the appellations of Didi, Gogo, and Lucky have been examined in detail, attention should be paid to Pozzo. If Pozzo is indeed the Godot whom they are awaiting, then analysis of his name will provide further evidence of this identity and of Beckett's creative imagination.

4. Advent

In the name of the former and of the latter and of the
holocaust. Allmen.

JAMES JOYCE

Once Pozzo's name is carefully examined, his position in
Beckett's dramatic scheme will be made clearer. It is but
a short step from the author's use of the play-within-the-
play to his creation of interchangeable character parts. This
is the whole point of Didi's and Gogo's little performances—
the pantomime and skit — in which they alternately assume
the roles of Lucky and Pozzo. Most critics have paid scant
attention to this kind of play-acting: they are for the most
part drawn to questions they believe to be of greater importance. In general, one type of Beckett criticism prefers an
abstract frame, viewing *Waiting for Godot* as a threnody on
the human condition. Another school of thought, in the mi-
nority despite support from the general literate public, leans
toward a concrete interpretation, treating the play as some
sort of religious statement.

While there are elements of truth in both of these critical
perspectives, adherents often tend not to heed Beckett's
warnings and they proceed at the risk of leaving undetected
some of the hidden resonances that endow this play with a
multidimensional, haunting appeal all its own. It is easy to
see how these lines of interpretation arose. On the one hand,
the play's seemingly Spartan dialogue and decor favor the
philosophical viewpoint, whereas its various religious symbols

are conducive to the spiritual interpretation. The double defect of these approaches is that they run the risk of not relating the philosophical or religious elements to the play's unfolding or to an understanding of the sources from which they derive.

In this chapter I would like to examine certain religious features found in the play as a point of departure, in order to demonstrate their relation to Beckett's dramaturgical attempt to make his characters interchangeable. Such matters are quite complex, and in order not to detract from the main theme of investigating onomastic techniques some of the supporting material has been relegated to critical appendixes. It must be restated here that Beckett has no religious axe to grind, no religious viewpoint to advocate or to denounce. He is more intrigued by the shape than by the content of the symbols to which he alludes. But his achievement will become more comprehensible only after these elements have been carefully elucidated. Critic Rolf Breuer in his study of the play has touched upon this specific point, and I will also try to show how and why Beckett has presented the characters in *Waiting for Godot* in a sophisticated Trinitarian dimension that renders them equal and different all at the same time.

According to the mysterious dogma of the Trinity, the three personalities of God are identifiable and unique. This is also true in the case of Beckett's tramps as related to Pozzo and ultimately to Godot and God. Now that the various resonances of the tramps' and Lucky's names have been identified, a close examination of Pozzo's should reveal how Beckett has nominally and dramatically linked these different elements in the unfolding of character development.

The religious dimensions of Gogo and Lucky have been observed and disputed by many critics. They have noted that Gogo once compares himself with Christ and that Lucky is literally a suffering servant. But insofar as religious dimensions are attributable to Beckett's figures, it remains Pozzo

who receives the bulk of critical attention. He has been
linked to God by a certain group of interpreters. This view
is part of a larger perspective that also holds Godot to be God.

Those who share this reading of the play find in the name
Godot a diminutive form of God. The name also conjures up
the French word *godenot,* a deformed man, and the only indication that Beckett has offered is that it is related to *godillot*
which means a large shoe. Whatever meaning the deprecatory
suffix holds, it usually leads toward a sort of theological
interpretation. It is difficult to avoid considering what Martin
Esslin terms the play's "basically religious quality." Religious
symbolism abounds throughout the piece. References to the
Old and New Testaments as such and to biblical quotations,
the crucifixion, even the barren and then blossoming tree,
all point to a religious framework of sorts. The religious
interpretations of the play are somewhat varied, tending
for the most part to emphasize the blind faith of Vladimir,
likening his plight to the seemingly endless sojourn of the
sinner in purgatory or to the Pascalian notion of man's misery
without God.

Notwithstanding Beckett's disclaimers about religious
meanings attributed to his play, the general public and not
a few critical observers prefer to view Godot as having something to do with God.[1] Theists and atheists alike are intrigued
and often baffled by the play's spiritual dimensions and implications. Invariably, critical discussions work their way back
to either supporting or denying the question of Godot's
identity with God. It is undoubtedly this feature of the
play that later propelled it into the public eye at about
the time that the notion of the "death of God" was beginning to gain recognition in the early 1960s.

Within the dimensions of the religious interpretations
there is a rather negative vision of Pozzo's role as Godot
which, reduced to the simplest equation, holds God to be
Godot, and Pozzo to be God; thus Pozzo emerges as Godot

and the horrific image of God. In the most succinct statement of this line of interpretation, Wylie Sypher plainly
asserts that "Pozzo, who does appear, would be, in the first
act, the terrible Old-Testament God, the tyrant-divinity,
and in the second act Pozzo would be a New Testament
God, manifesting himself as injured, crucified, helpless."[2]
This view of things points in a promising direction and it
has the virtues of simplicity and theological neatness. But
it leaves certain basic problems unresolved.

If Beckett merely wished to imply that God is a monster,
then the point of this play would be simplistic in the extreme. Beckett is not interested in such messages. But this
view of Pozzo and Godot, when seen in the light of character
transformation, does impose an entirely different focus on
the structure of the play, and its implications are worth ex-
ploring. A Christian critic, Jean Onimus examined this particular interpretation and found it an unworthy portrayal of
the monotheistic deity. He concluded that if Pozzo does
represent any God, it is certainly a prebiblical demiurge,
a Moloch or a Shiva, or perhaps an image created by the
poet to personify the evil he finds in the world. If the dif-
fering interpretations of God's nature could be limited to
the arguments of orthodox theology, the opinion of Onimus
might be acceptable. But a more useful insight can be gained
from investigating the recurring claims of certain classical
heresies, where central religious truths lie buried though
not forgotten. This line of inquiry can help explain the
strange religious aura that envelops *Waiting for Godot*.
It will also help explain the varied resonances aroused
by Pozzo's strange names.

It is not my intention to provide yet another trophy
for the collections of Godot hunters. As has already been
noted, Beckett's theater does not lend itself to the type of
static, classificatory criticism that produces definitive interpretations. His theater is purposely open and fluid, and his

characters are deliberately ambiguous as befits mythical creations, inviting the beholder to think about the multiple possibilities of appreciation at different levels of meaning. As in the works of Joyce the obscene here rubs shoulders with the sublime. Beckett's is above all a theater of implications rather than assertions. The playwright bids his audience to reflect on what it experiences. This feeling is partly lost at one point in the English version where the refrain "on attend Godot" is rendered "we're waiting for Godot." In the original an impersonal sort of expectation is thrust upon actor and audience alike; both feel drawn into the cycle of waiting.

One can get a glimpse of this play's embryonic beginning in a haunting line from Beckett's French poetry, written years before the play: "et on attend adverbe oh petit cadeau vide vide"[3] This suggests waiting for the Word (Verbum) made flesh, the suffering Christ who saves. Taken together, the two refrains "on attend adverbe" and "on attend Godot" imply the complementary stages of messianic waiting as chronologically expressed in the biblical Testaments. If such redemptive myths and eschatological patterns are present, then Sypher's view of Pozzo is partly justified.

But even this engaging equation of Pozzo and God is incomplete without reference to the contemporary theological and historical background that gave rise to the atmosphere in which the play was written. This accounts in large part for the deep resonances the play touched which launched it into spectacular popularity. *Waiting for Godot* is above all a play that aspires to universality, but it was not created in a vacuum; to a certain extent it is a reflection of the civilization that produced it. It could only have been written shortly after World War II, when the foundations of European culture lay in ashes. And only a guided examination of that spiritual background can put the play into perspective as a reflection of contemporary malaise. Such an analysis will illuminate Pozzo's bizarre name.

Waiting for Godot is a play about waiting and Godot. Its roots are set in a civilization that was based on monotheism. Judaism and Christianity are religions of waiting and expectation. In their most charitable moods some theologians think that the main difference between the two religions consists merely of the timing of the Messiah's arrival. In the broadest sense this may be true: Jews still waiting for the Messiah, Christians believing he has already come and will come again a second time. Because of the rival claims to the Messiah and the conflicting conceptions of his nature, each faith has accused the other of waiting for the wrong or a false Messiah. But the clashing viewpoints have to do with the psychology of the daughter religion's attitude toward the parent faith. The differences are not ill conceived nor misconstrued: they result from opposing world views that have shaped the foundations of Western civilization.

If one accepts the characterization of Pozzo as a god of sorts manifest among men, it will be interesting to discover that such a concept of a malevolent, brutal deity is implicit in the history of monotheistic religions, in its commentaries and legends, and that it is not merely the product of Beckett's imagination. Since Beckett presents the play in the form of a diptych, chronologically depicting what one may choose to interpret as the Messiah's successive appearances, it would be worthwhile to trace, briefly, the history of the Redeemer's manifestations to see where they have led, right up to modern times.

Christian critics have understandably been put off at the thought of identifying Pozzo with Godot, on the grounds that there is no biblical justification for such an embarrassing analogy. For the most part their reservations are well founded. However at the risk of making a complex work of art seem even more convoluted, I would like to suggest that such an image does exist, though not in orthodox Christianity. Exegetes of Beckett's work have been hard put at times

to explain his numerous references to biblical themes. This
confusion is understandable. But the critics have been reading
the wrong Bible in their attempts to draw parallels between
this play and Scripture. The general spirit and not a few details of *Waiting for Godot* are to be found in Christian apocryphal literature. Unable to explain Pozzo's mistreatment
of Lucky, interpreters tend to reject the problem of a malevolent God just as the Church Fathers were obliged to ex-
clude certain features and versions of biblical events, those
accounts which were relegated to that curious body of
unofficial biblical books called apocryphal.

In the French version of *Waiting for Godot* Pozzo is specifically leading his suffering servant to be sold at the market
of the Holy Savior. Pozzo's action has already been anticipated at the very beginning of the apocryphal *Acts of Thomas*.
Here the Lord wishes to send his reluctant disciple, Judas
Thomas, to India to preach the gospel there. The fact that
the Lord Jesus clearly refers to himself and his servant as
carpenters indicates the close bonds between them, even
a common identity. The Lord intends to sell Judas Thomas
to an Indian merchant who will take him back to his land
to spread the faith. More important than the sale itself is
the link between the Lord and his disciple, and once again
their names help point the way.

The author of this apocryphal book clearly intends to
repeat the curious legend that Jesus and Judas were twin
brothers, the latter being equally necessary through his
betrayal to bring about the divine redemptive sacrifice for
all mankind. That the heretical author intended to present
this odd relationship is emphasized by the disciple's name,
Judas Thomas, for Thomas is the Hebrew word for twin.
Character names reinforce character formation and function.
In the apocryphal *Gospel of Thomas* the author is called
Didymus Judas Thomas, Didymus being the Greek word
for twin. This name is deliberately redundant in order to

strengthen the view that Judas was the twin brother of Jesus.[4] And with these names in mind it would seem that Didi, too, is a twin.

In choosing a name like Didi for Vladimir, Beckett, when he chose to read philosophy, may also have been inspired by the stories concerning the life of the Alexandrian scholar called Didymus. A grammarian of immense learning and energy, Didymus was reputed to have written almost 4,000 books and was ridiculed for his contradictions. So prodigious was his output that he often forgot what he had written in earlier works and thus repeated himself in subsequent writings. There was nothing original about Didymus the writer: he epitomized the Alexandrian scholastic tradition and thus acted only as a preserver and transmitter of accumulated knowledge; as such he would lend himself to satire — a fitting model for Lucky, the modern intellectual with whom Vladimir-Didi can be compared. But Beckett is more interested in presenting Didi in a religious context than in a historical one. And the threads of this biblical message may once again be found in the apocryphal books.

In the orthodox Christian tradition, in the canonical books of the Bible, Judas is cast in the role of the arch-villain for his treachery toward Christ. But in the noncanonical books he is occasionally elevated almost to the rank of humanity's co-redeemer. Without his betrayal, so goes this logic, Christ would not have died to save humanity from sin. This bizarre though positive view of Judas as the twin brother of Jesus is reflected in theological thinking according to which Judas was damned not for betraying Christ but for hanging himself. The parallel stories of Christ's death on the cross and Judas's hanging on the tree are echoed in Didi's and Gogo's thoughts of committing suicide on the barren tree and later on the blossoming tree.

Shortly before their contemplation of suicide the tramps discuss the inconsistent Gospel narratives about the two thieves. They are rightly perplexed, like generations of biblical scholars who have been hard put to reconcile the conflicting details of this story and to make sense out of Christ's lavish promise to the good thief. Christ's boon to the good thief seems all out of proportion to his request. The good thief mentioned in Luke's Gospel asked Jesus to remember him once the divine kingdom was established: "And Jesus said unto him, Verily I say unto thee, Today shalt thou be with me in paradise." This saying, pronounced during the crucifixion agony, was supposed to have been uttered before the resurrection and transfiguration, those supreme moments in Christ's mission when eternal life would be granted to the penitent. In any event, Didi and Gogo puzzle over this text, and finally Didi suggests that they both repent. They obviously view themselves dimly in a similar context.

It is curious to note that in none of the four canonical Gospels are the two thieves named. Only in the apocryphal *Acts of Pilate* are they specifically named and there they are known as Dysmas and Gastas. Here Dysmas is treated as the good thief and Gastas as the bad, and if there is any nominal connection between them and Beckett's tramps, Dysmas will enter the kingdom of light and Gastas the realm of darkness. For after their deaths the legend has it that Joseph of Arimathaea reported that the body of Dysmas was not to be found and that of Gastas had turned into a dragon.

The vision of Estragon-Gogo-Gastas transformed into a dragon is not inappropriate in view of the tramps' first discussion of suicide which follows their talk about the two thieves. It is Estragon who is more enthusiastic at the prospect of suicide. In the original manuscript version of the play Beckett underscores Estragon's sacrificial character by naming him Lévy, in apparent reference to the priestly tribe of Levi. He is Baudelaire's executioner and victim, the priest and oblation all in one person. Out of boredom and the need to pass the time, Estragon, who calls himself Adam and compares himself to Christ, is eager to end their long vigil, to break the fatal circle of expectation and disappointment:

Estragon: Wait.
Vladimir: Yes, but while we're waiting.
Estragon: What about hanging ourselves?
Vladimir: Hmm. It'd give us an erection.
Estragon: (highly excited) An erection!
Vladimir: With all that follows. Where it falls mandrakes grow. That's
   why they shriek when you pull them up. Did you not know that?
Estragon: Let's hang ourselves immediately! (pp. 11-12)

The mandrake was thought to be an image in miniature of
a human being, and this is precisely what Gogo wishes to turn
into. He somehow recognizes his and Didi's diminished status
before the imposing presence of Pozzo and his slave. This
desire and others help explain the symbolic significance of
the mysterious plant in the play. As soon as Gogo becomes
aware of the weird legend of the mandrake, he is all the more
impelled to carry through his suggestion of suicide. He identifies himself with the odd plant which, according to folklore,
is watched over by the devil and is born of the sperm fallen
from hanged criminals. This detail links it to the theme of
the two thieves. As Didi says, the mandrake was reputed to
shriek upon being wrenched from the soil. At times a dog
was tied to this root and forced to pull it loose. The demon
spirit then passed from the plant into the dog and killed it.

In *Waiting for Godot* the reference to the mandrake occurs
in the first act in approximately the same relative position
as the reference in the second act to Didi's song about the
dog who dies and is buried at the foot of a little white cross.
This is not the first time that Beckett mentions the death
of a dog in his works. In *Watt* a dog is beaten to death for
stealing a piece of meat and is buried by some other dogs
under the wooden cross of a soldier. In *Molloy* and *All That
Fall* more variations on this theme reappear.[5]

Beckett and Joyce, among others, were greatly intrigued

by the suggestiveness of the mandrake. Its very name is stimulating. Although the exact origin of the word is obscure, English folk etymology connects it with the legend of a man-dragon. It has other significances as well that bear upon some of the arcane features of Beckett's work. Taken as a narcotic the juice of the plant affords release from this world's misery. The words uttered by Shakespeare's Cleopatra, "Give me to drink mandragora, that I might sleep out this great gap of time" (*Antony and Cleopatra*, 1.5.4), could easily have been those of Estragon who spends a great deal of time dozing and dreaming. Joyce, too, was keenly interested in this plant under the name of moly, and it is mentioned in the figure of Molly Bloom. And in *Molloy* it also surfaces with the same name: "Against such harmony of what avail the miserable molys of Lousse, administered in infinitesimal doses probably, to draw the pleasure out."[6] For Joyce and Beckett this mysterious plant is interwoven in pagan and Christian mythologies.

As a soporific the legendary mandrake has an ambivalent function which closely parallels the interchangeable roles assumed by Gogo as dragon and Christ, devil and God. In addition to being considered a diabolic narcotic it has also been associated in legend with the death wine, *morion,* which the Roman executioners would offer victims of crucifixion.[7] Given the ambivalent context of its mention in Beckett's play, it is almost impossible to tell whether the tramps wish to hang themselves to induce an erection or prefer to induce an erection in order to create mandrake roots in their own image, to make more homunculi like themselves who will continue their waiting, in diminished form, for Godot. Or perhaps they fail to commit suicide out of fear of reproducing themselves in the shape of mandrakes and thus prolonging their vigil throughout the aeons. The vagabonds do allude to previous adventures and existences which antedate their present situation. Gogo has been a poet (so he tells us) and he claims that he and Didi have been at the same spot before the tree sometime in the past.

Whatever the use of the mandrake here, it is definitely related to Gogo in particular in his multiple role of dragon, Christ, and Adam. These transmogrifications are not apparent on the stage, of course, and they are only dimly perceived in the text. Beckett's formal education was every bit as thorough as Joyce's, his knowledge of classical mythology just as profound, but he parted company with Joyce in the way he utilized this material.

Allusions to literature, religion, and mythology are equally present in Beckett's work except that they are even more disguised and muted in keeping with his aesthetic principle of ellipsis, litotes, and contracted expressiveness. Symbols allow him to identify, obliquely, the hidden levels that were meant to be partially concealed from the inquisitive reader. The myths ascribed to the mandrake plant are fantastic, sophisticated, and altogether in keeping with the roles he assigns to Gogo. There is one version that helps put into focus the overall spiritual climate of the play — the myth of Adam's rebirth, the new Adam reborn in Christ, an Adam come to life again on the very spot of the crucifixion, reconstituted from the mandrake plant and rekindled from the light of Gnostic religious beliefs.[8] The heart of this particular tradition helps explain the central part Pozzo plays in the process of character change.

In the ancient mystical tradition of Gnosticism — whose development paralleled, rivaled, and occasionally crossed that of Christianity — the meaning and message of Adam's birth, suffering, and rebirth held the key for understanding man's relationship to the divine scheme of things. In the apocryphal books of the New Testament the mandrake image and the cosmic struggle between demiurge and divinity are basically Gnostic in origin and inspiration. Their presence in *Waiting for Godot* suggests the framework for appreciating the play

and for identifying Beckett's use of religious myth to create
his own vision of human and divine relationships. This heterodox religious strain has been fleetingly observed in Beckett's
works; for example, John Pilling notes: "Beckett's attitude
is gnostic or manichean."[9] What is important here is that
Pilling links this line of thought to the biblical myth of Cain
and Abel. Its significance will become clearer after analysis
of Pozzo's name and its varied associations.

Before I continue this examination of Beckett's handling
of arcane religious imagery, two important viewpoints must
be briefly reemphasized. Beckett is indeed concerned with
the Christian scheme of things and he has chosen to parody
it indirectly, not through the orthodox but rather through
the heretical theological traditions. Beckett is not really
interested in refuting, and even less so in affirming, Christian
values. He is taken by Christianity's intellectual history, by
the patterns and shapes it has assumed. It would seem that
in the ancient Gnostic theogonies he found a ready-made
model for parody which he diverts to his own ends. But to
appreciate the two acts of *Waiting for Godot* as the double
disclosure of the biblical testaments, it is necessary to consider the thought of Marcion of Sinope, the most notorious
and influential dissident of Christian antiquity. Beckett's
views of God and man in his play are cast in the shadow
of Marcion's radical theology, a system of thought which
has had the widest and deepest implications for Christianity
and history right up to the present time. Marcion's works
and views are too complex to examine here (see Appendix
A for a brief résumé). It is enough to recognize that he
believed the God of the Old Testament to be the devil.[10]

At first glance such theological considerations seem somewhat removed from the criticism of *Waiting for Godot* and
from analysis of Pozzo's name. But concerning the theme
of personality change and interpenetration of character
it can be demonstrated that Beckett's odd couples submit

to a process of change similar to that advocated by Marcion's interpretation of scripture. This same diabolical pattern recurs throughout Joyce's work, and it is worth recalling that Pozzo does measure up to most of the characteristics of a fiendish deity. Thus Pozzo may appear to some to be a Colonel Blimp or a German officer berating his servant. To others he looks like the ringmaster or animal tamer from the circus. It should be noted in passing that the biblical scholar Rivkah Kluger observes that the earliest form of the word satan conveys the sense of one who persecutes, pursues, entraps, and puts fetters on his victim, all of which actions are amply demonstrated by Pozzo. From every angle he is diabolical.

The name Pozzo is the Italian word for well or hole, suggesting someone who has emerged from the depths of the earth, from an infernal region. The word also conjures up many other associations. *Pozzo* suggests *puzzo* meaning "stench" and *posso* meaning "I can" or "I am able." As a stench Pozzo may doubly serve as an amplification of Gogo's stinking feet and Didi's stinking breath. When Gogo calls him "Abel" he responds, and when Gogo calls Lucky "Cain" (p. 53) it is Pozzo instead who answers again to this name. Here the biblical roles of victim and aggressor are affirmed in one person. By responding to both names the crestfallen master underlines his interchangeable roles. By mentioning this myth Beckett also calls attention to the impossibility of understanding divine will, of fathoming why Yahweh accepted Abel's offering but spurned Cain's.

In answering as both Cain and Abel, Pozzo evokes in the English version the pathetic images of human impotence and potentiality. He says in effect that he can't and that he is able, that he is condemned to remain and to wander.[11] As a bilingual pun both associations are contained in the line from Dante — "Più non posso" — quoted by Beckett in his essay on Proust. In the play's first version Beckett has Pozzo utter these very lines in French: "Je n'en peux plus." As already noted the Italian words *pozzo* and *posso* respectively mean "well" and "I am able," and they correspond to the French *puits* and *je puis.* Beckett had long pondered this image of ambivalence. In *Murphy* he writes: "Humanity is a well with two buckets... one going down to be filled, the other coming up to be emptied" (p. 58). With these words in mind, the bonds linking the two couples are reaffirmed when Vladimir, observing Pozzo for the second time, says: "To all mankind they were addressed, those cries for help still ringing in our ears! But at this place, at this moment of time, all mankind is us, whether we like it or not" (p. 51).

Pozzo's name and character may have a historical derivation. In *The Shape of Chaos* the critic David Hesla writes: "It may be that Beckett took Lucky's name from Hegel, just as (and with a higher degree of probability) he may have taken Pozzo's name from Sartre" (p. 199). Hesla is referring here to the passage in *Being and Nothingness* where Sartre writes: "There exist however intermediates between states and qualities: for example, the hatred of Pozzo di Borgo for Napoleon although existing in fact and representing an affective, contingent relation between Pozzo and Napoleon the First was constitutive of the *person* Pozzo"[12]

If any historical personage is involved here it seems more likely that Beckett's imagination was aroused by the activities of the obstreperous Duke Joseph Pozzo di Borgo, a descendant of Napoleon's enemy, who was prominent in profascist movements in Paris during the 1930s when Beckett had already been residing in that city for some time. This Pozzo di Borgo (1890-1966) was one of the founders of the Croix de Feu and was arrested and imprisoned for his role in the right-wing terrorist group, La Cagoule. He was also president of the Institut anti-marxiste, often spoke at meetings of the Rassemblement anti-juif, and was a subscriber and benefactor of the notorious anti-semitic newspaper, *La Libre Parole.* In view of these activities this descendant of the prominent Corsican family would be a fitting model for the authoritarian fascistic personality assumed by Beckett's Pozzo. It is interesting to note in passing that echoes of his name seem to appear in *Finnegans Wake* (p. 609) as Pongo da Banza (Sancho Panza?) and as Porto da Brozzo (p. 560). Ten lines after this last reference we read, "The Corsicos? They are numerable."[13]

Beckett, as a student of Dante, probably culled this name from the *Divine Comedy* where *pozzo* is often used in the sense of a deep pit in hell. It is important to recall that the name Pozzo in Beckett's hands is an elaborate pun word permitting combinations of high and low meanings in a single utterance. Hugh Kenner observed that Beckett in his early fiction used the Italian name Belacqua with a double meaning. It is both a character from Dante and at the same time gutter Irish "Bollocky."[14] With Pozzo, Beckett uses the same technique as exemplified in the text when Didi and Gogo mispronounce his name:

Estragon: Ah! Pozzo...let me see...Pozzo...
Vladimir: Is it Pozzo or Bozzo?
Estragon: Pozzo...no...I'm afraid I...no...I don't seem to...
  Pozzo advances threateningly.
Vladimir: (conciliating). I once knew a family called Gozzo. The mother had the clap.
Estragon: (hastily). We're not from these parts, Sir. (p. 15)

It has been suggested that the Germanic pronunciation "Bozzo" might imply a Prussian arrogance in Pozzo's manner. But Beckett gives more attention to the Italian word *gozzo* which means "goiter." In relation to Pozzo's antics this also conjures up *gozzoviglia* which signifies "revelry, excessive eating." Beckett probably mentions it here as well in order to underline the strange bond between the master and the slave: two pages further in the text of the play Vladimir,

upon looking closer at Lucky's neck, exclaims: "Looks like
a goiter."

But Beckett is also using gutter Italian, for the name Gozzo
is close to the Neapolitan pronunciation of the noun *cazzo*
meaning "penis," a term which, according to the *Oxford
English Dictionary,* has been present in English under the
form "catso" since the early seventeenth century. Beckett's
use of the term is not so farfetched when one recalls that the
title of his earliest satirical tale, "Che sciagura," reappeared
in translation as "What a Misfortune" in his collection of
stories, *More Pricks than Kicks.* For this reason Federman and
Fletcher point out that Beckett was undoubtedly inspired by
the words of Voltaire's eunuch who at the end of chapter 11
of *Candide* laments: "Che sciagura d'essere senza coglioni."[15]
In the same line of punning Beckett probably had in mind
as well a celebrated phrase from another eighteenth-century
classic, Diderot's *Le Neveu de Rameau* (to which *Godot* bears
a certain resemblance): "Qui siedo sempre come un maestoso
cazzo fra due coglioni."[16] These words could easily sum
up almost the entire scenario of Beckett's play: a big penis
flanked by two blockheads.

In this scene Beckett follows Joyce in using "people to
stand for genitals, and geometrical symbols to stand for
people."[17] The three characters here form a triangle, each
point interrelated, an obscene parody of the Trinity and
the crucifixion scene with the two thieves at the side of the
Messiah. This interpretation of Pozzo's name neatly tallies
with the genital associations which have been clarified in
note 6 of this chapter.

It is most important to observe here the multiple resonances Beckett assigns to Pozzo's name which like those of
the other characters is a sophisticated pun. If Pozzo is derived
from Dante, from the names of a French fascist and a Proust-
ian model, and even from human anatomy, if he means all
this, then he means nothing; and nothing, of a very special

kind, is precisely what Beckett is trying to depict throughout his work.

This is a rather crucial segment of the play because here
the temperamental differences between the two tramps are
accentuated and shown to condition their perceptions of
reality. Vladimir does not recognize in Pozzo the Godot for
whom he thinks he is waiting. But Estragon always mistakes
the overbearing master for the stranger who is supposed to
save them. The flaw in Vladimir's perception does not allow
him to make the association that comes easily to his companion. Pozzo, in denying any resemblance to this Godot,
clearly indicates that some bond between them does exist.
Immediately after Didi and Gogo mispronounce his name,
Pozzo is quick to inform them:

> Pozzo: (halting). You are human beings none the less. (He puts on his
> glasses.) As far as one can see. (He takes off his glasses.) Of the same
> species as myself. (He bursts into an enormous laugh.) Of the same
> species as Pozzo! Made in God's image! (p. 15)

This is precisely what Vladimir does not wish to see. From
the very beginning it is quickly established that Vladimir is
supposed to be the intellectual, the thinking member of the
pair insofar as he does most of the reflecting for the two.
Estragon is presented as the dullard who has trouble understanding why his friend insists on keeping the vigil. In this
line of characterization Beckett adheres closely to the tradition of French classical comedy, as perfected by Molière, in
which humble beings of secondary importance often perceive,
through their innate common sense and folk wisdom, great
simple truths which their sophisticated betters are incapable
of recognizing. Molière, too, was greatly influenced early in
his career by the commedia tradition, but unlike this playwright Beckett has retained all the brutality demonstrated
in the Italian comic tradition.

After this point in the play Pozzo and Lucky exit and later

reappear in the second act under drastically altered conditions which Wylie Sypher has characterized as a transformation from the brutal God into a hysterical Christ figure who bears all the suffering of humanity. And for the third time Estragon then thinks he has recognized Godot. Once again the theological and historical development of this transformation should briefly be considered in order to show how it fits into the sequential unfolding of the play.[18]

Beckett's portrayal of Pozzo's second coming is reminiscent of Nietzsche's attitude toward Christ. Altruism, pity, repentence, in Nietzsche's view, are simply masks for self-abnegation, guilt, and impotence. Self-flagellation involves collective masochism, poisoning all that it touches, turning man to fanaticism and sickness. Early in the first act Estragon innocently asks Vladimir if they are linked to Godot. As soon as Vladimir ridicules his comrade's question, Pozzo enters holding a rope around Lucky's neck which visibly symbolizes man's bond to his master and creator. In the second act the same couple comes back, except that this time Pozzo has changed drastically, or appears to have changed: one can never be sure about Pozzo for he is a liar. Nevertheless, he says he is blind, his rope restraining Lucky is now definitely shorter, and the master's wretched state seems to approximate that of the slave. This transformation implies the narrowing of the gap between creator and creature. When the tramps approach them they are caught as if in a net, and all four find themselves on the ground. Eventually Pozzo and Lucky get up and march away, and Vladimir and Estragon resume their vigil. Here the play ends. The beholder is left with the feeling that the two vagabonds, blissfully ignorant of all that has befallen them, will continue to await the future arrival of Godot.

There is little tragic about Vladimir and Estragon that meets the eye. Outwardly they have not changed, at least not very much. Basically, their attitude toward Godot's

heralded arrival is pathetic. Either he never shows up or he
appears in two successive guises and remains almost completely unrecognized. One could easily subscribe to the opinion that this play represents the death certificate of hope,
but Estragon and Vladimir seem unaware of the dead end.
They do carry on, and the aim of the play is thus reflected
in their absurd expectations. If they admit the folly of their
waiting, hope will evaporate and they will find themselves
in hell. They would then have to be more serious about their
repeated attempts at suicide. Their irrational vigil enables
them to enter into the illusion that the next time Godot will
appear in a recognizable shape.

Their protracted attentiveness does not really imply the
impossibility of Godot's arrival: it may even intimate on a
more profound level the need to adhere to an "as if" philosophy of contingency, to go on believing in the ideal even
though its realization may be too terrible to behold.[19] This
deferred consummation underscores the genius of Jewish
Messianism. The Messiah figure is central but not essential
to Judaism, whereas all Christian theology rests upon his
elusive nature and long-awaited return. In Christianity and
Islam a messianic figure of sorts has already arrived and his
return is ardently awaited by the faithful. For the Jews, on
the other hand, this arrival either causes or accompanies terror, disappointment, and, in the words of Gershom Scholem,
"a theory of catastrophe." Within Judaism itself, consider for
example the careers of Bar Kokhba, Sabbatai Sevi, and Jacob
Frank, all of which brought the greatest moments of suffering, apostasy, and disillusionment. The danger and hence
reluctance to encounter the Messiah, the awaited one, are
reflected in the talmudic prayer: "May he come, but I do
not want to see him."[20] Clearly the Messiah is more important before than after his arrival.

Is Pozzo really the awaited one? It is easy to see how he
could be taken to represent the image of a flawed deity. How-

ever, Beckett's dramaturgical psychology is too sophisticated for such a simplistic equation. Pozzo as a character is extremely complex — hence the significance of the resonances conjured up by his odd name. He may indeed suggest the advent of the awaited one, since Gogo often identifies him as Godot. The arrival of Godot would be as overwhelming as the arrival of the Messiah. Didi waits for Godot but he really does not wish to meet him. Such an encounter would force him to come to terms with the self and its true relationship to the other. This Didi wishes to avoid.

In the overall structure and rhythm of the play, Beckett has evoked and parodied a Trinitarian movement that proceeds from historical biblical manifestations of God to the threshold of the third future era in which the Holy Spirit will appear once again, thus completing the divine unfolding of the Godhead. In 1932 Beckett finally abandoned his teaching position at Trinity College, Dublin, in a symbolic and real rejection of his entire way of life, country, and ultimately language, in order to strike out anew in that France soon to be at war which he preferred to an Ireland at peace. Beckett himself was never particularly religious, but the personal anomaly of being a Protestant Irishman living in a Catholic area may have caused him to give up the scene of the fratricidal strife and stultifying provincialism endemic to that wretched isle. His few comments about both communities reveal nothing but scorn. Viewed in this light the play might be considered as a rejection of both the cruel puritan God and the hysterical Catholic God of his homeland were it not for the fact that Beckett's theater is singularly ahistorical, apolitical, and nonnationalistic.

Apparent simplicity of content and presentation, however, should not lead one to discount the influence of historical and political circumstances on the formation of the playwright's imagination, especially during his sojourns in France and Germany where he personally witnessed the disintegration of that higher Western civilization to which he and Joyce had been drawn. This period on the continent during the rise of Nazism may have influenced the curious open ending of *Waiting for Godot*. Richard Ellmann writes that Beckett tried to alert Joyce to the rise of Nazism. And during the German occupation of France, Beckett was almost arrested by the Gestapo for his work in the Resistance. For this reason alone Kenner's latest appraisal of Pozzo seems especially pertinent: "We can easily see why a Pozzo would be unnerving. His every gesture is Prussian. He may be a Gestapo official clumsily disguised."[21] Not quite, however. This view would limit Beckett's inspiration too closely to a specific concrete occurrence or type, and this Beckett usually avoids. But Kenner is not far off the mark. The connection of Pozzo with an authoritarian personality unfolds itself on a more profound level which is consistent with the main theme of waiting as developed in this play.

There is no third act for *Waiting for Godot* on the stage; it is merely implied by the continuous waiting. This choice on Beckett's part underlines his dramatic genius.[22] If he had included a third act on the stage, he would have been forced to expose the general direction that his play is taking; he would have had to show exactly how Didi and Gogo finally come to grips with the implications of this waiting. Instead Beckett prefers to leave the audience in a state of suspense and anxiety concerning the actions of Didi and Gogo at last faced with the truth about their situation.

This conjecture — the possible third arrival of the awaited one — is not without precedent in the theological development of the messianic idea, especially in the peculiar political shape that it took during the 1930s in Germany. Once again certain themes of modern theological speculation provide a focal point to illustrate the implications of messianic expectation and they help to explain the connections between politics and theater that probably contributed to Beckett's unique dramatic vision. It is no accident that critics have taken Pozzo to be the embodiment of a Germanic authoritarianism. Of course the specifics of his stage presence are not German at all. What links him to this period of history is his attachment to the form of lordly domination that was so successfully exploited by Hitler. The theme was effectively satirized by Charlie Chaplin, and Beckett was undoubtedly impressed by this master of the silent cinema comedy (See Appendix B).

It is not, to be sure, possible to attribute absolutely the origins of Beckett's masterpiece to the historical myth of a secularized Messiah. Yet it seems rather unlikely that he should have remained unaffected during the formative years spent on the continent by such political, historical, and aesthetic factors. In view of his association with Joyce, who invoked the messianic myth at the beginning of *Ulysses,* it would not be unreasonable to assume that Beckett was familiar with this notion of expectation in literature.

Given the Trinitarian frame of *Waiting for Godot,* Beckett's play lends itself to such an interpretation. Acts 1 and 2 present Pozzo, three times taken for Godot, as the embodiment of the Old and New Testament visions of God.[23] As analysis of these characters' names has demonstrated, it would be unwise to limit them exclusively to any one type of function. This is why Beckett treated them as puns and endowed them with antithetical senses. The multiple and often contradictory name meanings are reinforced by the characters' role exchanges. The import of the onomastic relationship is dimly perceived by Gogo and initially denied by Didi.

Beckett declined to pursue the Trinitarian current to its logical conclusion in this play. As he mentioned to Israel Shenker during an interview: "One act would have been too little and three acts would have been too much."[24] In so doing he held fast to his basic dramatic design and intent which constantly strives, in his own words, to avoid definition. This emphasis on ambiguity is the dramatist's way of underscoring what he perceives to be the fundamental uncertainty at the root of human existence. On the aesthetic level, this sense of insecurity is reflected in the sounds of the character names themselves. These appellations, especially Pozzo's, emphasize the plural aspects of personality development. Pozzo's name is doubly significant because it serves as a link between Godot and Gogo. Its assonance suggests a reappraisal is in order to appreciate the nature of the relationship between the two tramps.

5. Conclusion

Un jour il se verra...
SAMUEL BECKETT
Pour finir encore

The main function of character names in Beckett's play is
to suggest the multiple dimensions of dramatic roles. At the
heart of *Waiting for Godot* is the double desire to recognize
and to ignore the awaited one, to see and not to see, to affirm
the will to exist and to die. The ability to exist as more than
one person at a time is the chief reason for the exchange of
character roles and their shifting names. Beckett has charged
his clowns to remain in perpetual conflict in order to emphasize the basic strain of agnosticism which frustrates them and
their beholders in the audience. Because of these equally balanced contradictory impulses the play, then, seems to end at
an impasse.

If these names are deliberately misleading, so too is much
of the dialogue. The delayed gratification and the postponed
arrival were announced from the outset by Vladimir's mis-
quotation: "Hope deferred maketh the something sick, who
said that?" (p. 8). He has in mind the words from Proverbs
13:12, "Hope deferred maketh the heart sick: but when the
desire cometh, it is a tree of life." The desire finally material-
ized when the puny tree on stage sends out a few leaves. Yet
the stalemate persists, nothing is consummated, and so the
second act appears to be a repetition of the first. However,
a very subtle transformation has occurred, one which mainly

affects Didi and his way of viewing his position. In this deli-
cate shift of emphasis and perception the central mystery of
Godot's nature and function is crystallized.

Godot is not only an abstract image of hope that allows
the tramps to pass the time. He does fulfill that role but his
true purpose and identity are more awesome and immediate,
and, as we have seen, this has been perceived throughout,
though rather inconclusively, by Gogo. Each time Pozzo
makes his entrances and exits Gogo believes him to be Godot.
Even on the third and final assertion of this intuition toward
the end of act 2 Didi still reprimands his companion, but now
with a telling difference:

Vladimir: It seemed to me he saw us.
Estragon: You dreamt it. *(Pause.)* Let's go. We can't. Ah! *(Pause.)* Are
    you sure it wasn't him?
Vladimir: Who?
Estragon: Godot.
Vladimir: But who?
Estragon: Pozzo.
Vladimir: Not at all! *(Less sure.)* Not at all! *(Still less sure.)* Not at all!
Estragon: I suppose I might as well get up. *(He gets up painfully.)* Ow!
    Didi!
Vladimir: I don't know what to think any more. (p. 58)

This is a revealing confession coming from someone who
has been acting like the self-appointed thinker of the pair,
the one who was confident of his beliefs and expectations.
From the point of view of self-knowledge and recognition
this avowal constitutes a major chink in the protective armor
in which Didi is enveloped. His smugness has been weakened,
but the nagging question remains, To what avail?

This doubt on Didi's part presupposes something to be
weakened, some solid convention between characters that
has either broken down or stands in part exposed. Though
Vladimir, before this final confession, assumed almost an
air of omniscience and confidence about their vigil, he will

not be able to sustain it as before. He now leaves too many things unsaid or approaches them obliquely. And the ultimate reason, as far as Beckett is concerned, is aesthetic as well as psychological. The suggestion, the tentative explanation, that I have to offer is an *argumentum ex silentio*. Beckett's character names and the play itself appear to allow him a good deal of flexibility and ambivalence in the presentation of myth. But it is also true that he is restrained by the dramatic norms that directly affect his sensibility and the development of his characters. And this aesthetic circumspection makes every word uttered by his creatures a special occasion for simultaneously allowing the emergence and the suppression of dangerous knowledge.

It has been observed that the four major figures in this play, thanks to their protean names, represent certain aspects of a fragmented personality. This focus of attention on a generic self is undoubtedly the keystone of the aesthetic structure of *Waiting for Godot*. Critical views, of course, on the formalistic significance of the play vary considerably. In an insightful but desultory essay Eva Metman, for example, offers a Jungian interpretation of the play complete with an alchemical key to identify the various stages traversed by the self on its circuitous journey toward fulfillment. Metman rightly comments that this process of individuation is "an exceptionally long drawn-out one."[1] She contends that the development of Beckett's characters closely parallels the evolution of the soul, of the dismembered human image that Jung elaborately traces in his writings on psychology and alchemy.

Metman remarks, however, that Beckett shrinks from completing the cycle, from allowing the emergence of a "conscious gnosis." Beckett uses combinations of Christian and Gnostic symbols to suit his own dramatic purposes. But Beckett is not a Gnostic in the literal sense of the term, inasmuch as he denies the possibility of certain knowledge. Metman's explanation tries to account for the characters' uncompleted state by suggesting that the human scheme of things is too complex to allow for so neat a solution. And up to this point her view is accurate. Her opinion is based upon the theory that the "four unrelated fragments of personality in Godot" cannot achieve reconciliation. Yet the persistent questions remain: Why is this impossible, and Are the fragments really unrelated?

In his psychological study of the play G. C. Barnard offers a comprehensive examination of the personality split in Beckett's theater. This book still falls somewhat short of providing an answer to the question of why the split is maintained, however. Barnard observes that the two tramps "are not really separate persons but two halves of one man."[2] Though this is an accurate assessment it does not completely account for the presence of that other couple. Barnard's description of the schizoid split is valid, but perhaps it does not go far enough.

Pozzo and Lucky also exchange roles. Midway through the first act the master acknowledges his bond to his slave when he proclaims: "Remark that I might just as well have been in his shoes and he in mine. If chance had not willed otherwise" (p. 21). And toward the end of act 2 he recalls, again alluding to Lucky's name and status: "I woke up one fine day as blind as Fortune" (p. 55). Lucky, in the person of chance and fortune, determines the fate of Pozzo. Onomastically Beckett underscores this link through his careful choice of names.

The divided personality and its reuniting also transcend the two couples. Pozzo and Lucky do not arrive simply for the sake of dramatic contrast with Gogo and Didi but rather for the purpose of reflecting them. Professor Eugene Webb's view of this aspect of the play comes close to the interpretation I have been trying to develop. He too perceives the benefits gained by the tramps' contemplation of the other couple: "If what they seek from Godot is what Lucky has already found, then the emptiness of their hope is obvious, at least to the audience. Fortunately for their peace of mind, however, it is not obvious to them."[3] Close examination of this aspect of the play would show that the full implications of the association with the master and slave is surely not obvious to Gogo. But Didi, in the end, is another matter.

Throughout this study the individual character names have been exhaustively analyzed. Now it is fitting to compare the four names in order to show what the two couples truly have in common. By the assonance of their names Didi is related to Lucky and Gogo to Pozzo and ultimately Godot. Pozzo and Lucky are the *Doppelgänger* of the tramps, whose roles are grotesquely amplified and reversed in their successive appearances.

The relationship and identification are indirectly acknowledged when Didi says, "All mankind is us, whether we like it or not," and when Gogo remarks of Pozzo, "He's all humanity" (p. 51). Beckett never allows his clowns to realize the full import of these sayings. In the consecutive moments of the everyday life Gogo vaguely intuits (and forgets) the true link between master and slave, matter and spirit, time and space, instinct and intelligence. It falls upon Didi, however, to contemplate the nature and implications of this relationship that is echoed throughout their various metamorphoses and name changes.

Didi ultimately gets a glimpse of himself in Lucky. Otherwise what is the point of the pantomime and playlet and Didi's concluding gesture on the play's last page when he takes off Lucky's hat, peers inside and puts it on again? Here he belatedly resigns himself to a role that is akin to Lucky's. Didi finally manages to take that look at the self and he perceives an abyss. Fortunately for him, his companion's memory is more defective than his own. Gogo can blurt out but not fathom this transcendent affinity between the couples. The burden falls back upon Didi. This responsibility to understand their situation remains with him, and his rather late avowal of doubt relating to Pozzo's identity takes on a complex aspect, one with many possible interpretations.

In his detailed study of the philosophical influences on Beckett's imagination, David Hesla comes closest to the core of Godot's function. By way of Hegel and his terrible discovery that "the other is not only out there in the world but also in here, as an integral and essential element of the self," Hesla manages to draw the thrust of perception back from the outer to the inner realms of existence. But here the identification remains still incomplete.[4] Hesla identifies Godot impersonally as some sort of category of "Time Future." This is one function that the awaited one does fulfill. Other critics see him as a dramatic pretext to give the tramps hope and keep them waiting. Didi thus realizes the nature of Godot's time schedule and again one recalls the full force of his words. "It's already tomorrow" (p. 50). In French he says: "Nous sommes déjà demain," a phrase which more strikingly underlines his reluctant identification with Godot.

Beckett's time scheme has been studied by many critics. Here the past and future seem to hold little meaning: the past is quickly forgotten and the future is utterly unknowable. Only the fleeting sense of the present permits any focal point, a point of reference and feeble orientation. But even the idea of the present is deceptive; it is the past too rapidly merging with the future, the two existing simultaneously. Thus Didi laments at the end: "Astride of a grave and a difficult birth. Down in the hole, lingeringly, the grave-digger puts on the forceps. We have time to grow old" (p. 58).[5]

This kind of present conveys the apprehension of the void, like the abyss that always haunted Pascal, following him forever throughout his life. Godot may stand for many things not the least of which is an unwanted symbol of self-awareness apprehended and refracted through the affinity, recognition and interchanges of the past and future. Above all else, on the aesthetic level, the significance of Godot is revealed

through his name in connection with those of the other characters. Godot never comes because he is always and already
there. Didi and Gogo are waiting for themselves, and Lucky
and Pozzo are transmogrified mirror images to help them,
especially Didi, to recognize this actual ground of being.

In view of Didi's final declaration of doubt and inability
to think, the erstwhile philosopher of the pair is now forced
into a posture of self-deception.[6] Since it seems safe to assume that to all appearances their waiting for Godot will
continue as before, one is now led to conclude that Didi's
part constitutes a form of defense mechanism.[7] He is now
playing two roles at once and seems to know it. Where the
play superficially reflects the antics of four separate individuals or two distinct couples, Didi's recognition, his new-found
knowledge, reduces their clowning to the dimensions of a
monodrama. Didi almost comes to perceive that their various
postures are roles played by the same basic personality at war
with itself and engaged in a form of self-deception akin to
Sartrean bad faith.[8]

The contradictory demands of reality and illusion oblige
Didi to prolong this *folie à deux.*[9] To do otherwise would
require that he admit his reversed role, his inferior status in
the pair. The two arrivals of Pozzo and Lucky stand as indirect notice to Didi about the real nature of his relationship
to his companion. The two couples are not unrelated but
rather unconnected and disjointed. Theirs is a bond that
remains to be sealed, but not if Didi can help it.[10]

This ambiguity of intentions fits into Beckett's dramatic
design. By declining to explicate his aims, he deliberately sets
his characters (and the critics) at odds with one another. His
major play contains two or more fields of action which suggest that it should not be viewed as pessimistically as is usually the case. Beckett did realize Flaubert's wish to write a book
about nothing, but he knew that this nothingness must be
cast in some concrete shape. The form that he found most

suitable was derived from the commedia dell'arte set in a twentieth-century music-hall decor and suffused with just enough ambiguity so as not to permit any single definitive evaluation to emerge. This is the main reason for the variable character names.

Insofar as philosophical considerations and elements are combined with dramatic purpose, Beckett tends to cast these creative tensions in a struggle that falls somewhere between the thinking of Vico and of Descartes. Beckett is no more a philosopher than Joyce is, but he cannot resist the temptation to offer "Vicous circles" and negate them with Cartesian doubt where meaning tends to reinforce and cancel meaning at every turn.[11] Like Montaigne's portraits of Democritus and Heraclitus, the laughing and the weeping philosophers, Beckett's characters and their names are the battleground of unresolved conflicts.[12] And like Montaigne, Beckett would readily have them offer one candle to Saint Michael and another to his dragon.

In spite of, or perhaps because of, his deliberate obfuscation, Beckett's linguistic and dramatic virtuosity still remain within the aesthetic norms that he outlined in his early essay on Proust: "The artistic tendency is not expansive, but a contraction."[13] Whether the sparse dramatic decor is due to his choice of the French language and its classical tradition, to his Protestant upbringing, or to a rejection of the natural poetizing tendencies of the mother tongue and the influence of Joyce it is impossible to tell with certainty. And however related his work seems to be to that of Cervantes and Joyce, by his own ruthless economy of expression Beckett in this masterpiece is also able to evoke a grandiose range of associations all compressed within the delineation of the solitary and elusive self.

All this playing with the notions of reality and illusion, this clowning self-mockery and parody, is like what goes on in Cervantes and Joyce. But Beckett contrasted his work with

Joyce's thus: "The more Joyce knew the more he could. He's tending toward omniscience and omnipotence as an artist. I'm working with impotence, ignorance."[14] Unlike the simulation of life in the works of his mentors, Beckett offers radical doubt and uncertainty as the basis for conflict and creativity. The effect of his work is the result of an accumulation of details designed to destroy any handy key meant to unlock what are taken to be its secrets.

This has led to the numerous misunderstandings that Beckett's work, in the playwright's view, has been subjected to. *Waiting for Godot* may constitute a statement on the human condition or on the agony of lost faith, but ultimately it is a play created to lead the reader or beholder through various labyrinths to a dead end. This is why Beckett found the commedia tradition a suitable vehicle for his endeavors. Now you see it; now you don't. The clowns' multiple identities, highlighted by pantomime and name changes, reveal and obscure that substantial nothingness that occupies their waking and sleeping moments.[15]

However much certain features may resemble or even be inspired by Joycean fiction, Beckett has entirely different intentions. The works of the two authors propel themselves in opposite directions. Joyce is the poet of verbal explosion, Beckett of verbal implosion, or as Hugh Kenner puts it, Joyce is the "comedian of the inventory" whereas Beckett is the "comedian of the impasse."[16] With Beckett, language really never runs away with itself in the final analysis. Through prodigious effort and discipline he almost always remains its master despite an occasional disclaimer on his part. And for all the gloom and despair in his work Beckett is above all a comic writer: "the first great academic clown since Sterne."[17] Hence the vast erudition lurking behind the deceptively simple though bizarre character names. The myriad role exchanges and name changes experienced by his clowns could suggest an ineffable intimation of the divine reached by way of a modern *via negativa*. But once again it must be stressed that Beckett is not really interested in presenting religious themes per se in his work.[18] Those elaborate symbols are pretexts for the artist to create something which is its own end.

There is no easy way to appreciate *Waiting for Godot*. Those critics who seem to wrap it up in a neat package do so at the risk of overlooking its richness. The attempt offered in this study of the playwright's onomastic techniques should shed some light on his extraordinarily complex imagination. Beckett is not always leading his public on a wild-goose chase. Though his more ambitious works are often devised like elaborate puzzles, they offer no solutions. The author's skepticism remains radical. As far back as 1929 Beckett gave voice to his fundamental Pyrrhonism in the opening lines of his essay on Joyce: "The danger is in the neatness of identifications. The conception of Philosophy and Philology as a pair of nigger minstrels out of the *Teatro dei Piccoli* is soothing like the contemplation of a carefully folded ham-sandwich."[19]

Beckett's own oxymoronic minstrels depart to lead and mislead, to unsettle with laughter, to keep us constantly aware of that fundamental word in their creator's vocabulary, "perhaps." Their task is to keep us forever open to the implications of the contrived ambiguity of his art. The various resonances associated with their names have been carefully examined in this study. But it is important to remember that these appellations are not limited to allegorical or symbolic meanings in the traditional sense of these terms. The reason these characters seem to have so many names is that they are designed to disintegrate into formlessness. In having so many designations they often appear to be nameless. Regarding this technique Lawrence Harvey observes that "every time one tries to make words express something other than themselves 'ils s'alignent de façon à s'annuler mutuellement?"[20] This is why the names are so suggestive: they are meant to cancel themselves out. It is the stamp of Beckett's genius that as pure sounds these names, through their respective assonances, aesthetically imply the kind of role reversals that have been noted in analyzing the various themes taken from theatrical, religious, and political history.

The affinity with other masterpieces, the oblique references to mythology, religion, and philosophy, these are all a part of what Beckett calls "the spray of phenomena." The meanings multiply, they shift ground, they accumulate with each reading. This kind of growth takes place in all great literary works: a particular pattern momentarily arises only to yield to another multiplicity of associations radiating out into other dimensions. That Beckett has such a pulsating design in mind is exemplified by Pozzo's famous soliloquy on the cosmos delivered in the middle of act 1:

An hour ago (he looks at his watch, prosaic) roughly (lyrical) after having poured forth even since (he hesitates, prosaic) say ten o'clock in the morning (lyrical) tirelessly torrents of red and white light it begins to lose its effulgence, to grow pale (gesture of the two hands lapsing by stages) pale, ever a little paler, a little paler, until (dramatic pause, ample gesture of the two hands flung wide apart) pppfff! finished! it comes to rest. But — (hand raised in admonition) — but behind this veil of gentleness and peace night is charging (vibrantly) and will burst upon us (snaps his fingers) pop! like that! (his inspiration leaves him) just when we least expect it. (Silence. Gloomily.) That's how it is on this bitch of an earth. (p. 25)

Like the steady-state model of the continuous creation in the universe, Waiting for Godot appears to expand and contract rhythmically in linguistic explosions and implosions. Like the black holes of highly condensed matter observed at the far reaches of the universe, expression here yields to impression in a never-ending cycle.[21] This emphasis on clowning and a dialectical pattern of character growth is dictated in part by Beckett's wish to parody the assumptions of Western thought and sensibilities.[22] But parody is also a proper form of homage.

More important, the names of these clowns, through the various associations examined here, aesthetically bear the hallmark of genius. Naming-day in no-man's-land never ends for Beckett's anonymous heroes.

APPENDIX A.
Theological Impact of Marcion

Marcion was greatly influenced by the writings of Luke. It is therefore pertinent to note that according to E. Earle Ellis "The third and most pervasive motif in Luke-Acts is the relationship of Judaism and Christianity, and the awful fact of the Jews' rejection of their Messiah is continually brought to the attention of the reader. The principal purpose of the Lukan writings very likely is to be found in this dominant theme"(*The Gospel of Luke* [London: Thomas Nelson, 1966], p. 59; see also Charles Talbert, *Luke and the Gnostics* [Nashville, Tenn.: Abingdon Press, 1966]). Beckett is concerned with this Gospel and perhaps he intended to mention it to reinforce Vladimir's rejection, however unconscious, of the Messiah figure, Godot.

Alfred Loisy, the great French biblical scholar, has termed Marcion the most dangerous heretic ever expelled from orthodox Christianity (*Histoire et mythe* [Paris: Nourry, 1938], p. 106). Marcion was the son of a bishop who excommunicated him on charges of immorality. Early in the second century he formulated the most extreme challenge ever posed to Christian theology. In brief his doctrine, based partly on a form of Gnostic philosophy, demanded a complete separation between the Old and the New Testaments. Up to a point Jewish thinkers might have agreed with him, for they had no desire to see their scripture twisted to fit Christian purposes. But the unique feature of Marcion's theology was his charac-

terization of the Jewish God as a demiurge, a contentious god
of evil, responsible for man's suffering in the world, whereas
the Christian God represented all that was good and merciful.
Marcion was impressed by Paul's rejection of the Mosaic law
and he carried his denunciation to its logical conclusion, or
reduced it to the absurd, in postulating that the church was
mistaken in retaining the old Jewish canon as part of its literature.

With singleminded zeal Marcion accepted only the Gospel
of Luke and edited it to conform to his own theology.
Marcion also founded a church which was widespread and
influential throughout nascent Christendom, and it is suspected that the first Latin translation of the Bible may have
been made by one of his disciples. Marcion treated the God
of the Jews as a capricious, vindictive, and vicious tyrant
whose chief delight was annihilating his enemies and punish-
ing his own backsliding followers.

The early church was faced with a dilemma: it easily recognized that its own dejudaizing campaign had been carried
too far by the likes of Marcion. One may trace this general
trend from the Synoptic Gospels, which deal with the life
of Jesus, to the Evangel of John which, imbued with certain
Gnostic tendencies and a more negative treatment of Jews,
glorifies the Christ. John in his gospel (8:44) and Marcion,
writing at about the same time, refer to the God of the Jews
as a devil. Marcion and his disciples only carried it one step
further by implying that Christ must have been sacrificed by
an evil god. The primitive church, of course, was aware of the
direction in which it was moving, but it also realized that a
complete break with its Judaic heritage would undermine the
whole prophetic basis of its own messianic claims. Therefore
Marcion was denounced, and in response to his challenge the
church was forced to draw up the official canon of its own
scripture as well as retaining the biblical canon already established by the Jews.

But in defeat Marcion had his greatest victory. Although

the church succeeded in officially repudiating his extreme anti-Judaism, it could never completely divest itself of the nagging assumption that the God of the Jews was really the God of evil. In orthodox Christian thought the doctrine of the devil was formally assigned to the malevolent spirit, the devil as opposed to Yahweh; but under the influence of a defeated Gnosticism and paganism, Christians were still tempted to see the world and cosmos almost equally divided between these rival divinities. For the past two centuries Marcion has been considered a precursor of modern biblical criticism, and his influence is widespread, particularly his radical rejection of the Old Testament and its image of God.

It is not surprising that even the casual reader of the Old Testament might occasionally be struck by the thought that Yahweh was originally a demonic God (see Rivkah Schärf Kluger, *Satan in the Old Testament* [Evanston, Ill.: Northwestern University Press, 1967], p. 10). Even the ancient Hebrews were perplexed by the God who "creates light and darkness." Some Jews today take pride in asserting that in their religion the devil occupies an insignificant place compared with the honors rendered him in Christianity. One might add that with a God like Yahweh, who needs a devil? Freud and Reik in their early studies noted a certain confusion and ambivalence in the primitive stages of the Hebrew religion. The concept of a unique divine personality is the main achievement of the Old Testament, but this notion only took shape once the cult of Yahweh was firmly established. For further discussion, see Theodor Reik, *Der Eigene und der fremde Gott* (Leipzig: Internationaler Psychoanalytischer Verlag, 1923), p. 149; Sigmund Freud, "Neurosis of Demoniacal Possession," in his *Collected Papers* (London: Hogarth Press, 1953), 4:450; and Ernest Jones, *On the Nightmare* (London: Hogarth Press, 1931), p. 157. For the same theme in Joyce see Cixous, *L'Exil de James Joyce ou l'art remplacement* (Paris: Grasset, 1968), pp. 619-20.

At this point of religious development, according to

Theodor Reik, the triumphant theology became more sophisticated and displaced upon the vanquished cults whatever
malevolent forces may have been originally inherent in its
own deity. Thus in defeat the fertility cults of Canaan became the abominations of Leviticus. By this same process
the old God, Yahweh, would be relegated to the status of
a vanquished deity whose power, especially in popular imagination, would be equated with that of the devil. See Paul
Carus, *The Devil and the Idea of Evil* (New York: Land's End
Press, 1969), p. 71.

In Christian mythology the devil's importance is considerably augmented and the evil one's power is traced back to
the fallen angel who dared to aspire to the greatness of God.
Despite the church's official teaching and occasional admoni-
tions, it is easy to see how the popular imagination, nurtured
on this theology, came to confuse the Jewish God with Satan.
The growth and development of Christianity entailed an
increasing awareness of the devil's distinct existence and
responsibility for the world's misfortunes, and in the popular
mind the Jew was identified as his emissary. On this tradition
see Joshua Trachtenberg, *The Devil and the Jews* (New Haven,
Conn.: Yale University Press, 1953). This theological background is essential to an understanding of the religious frame
and symbols that appear in *Waiting for Godot.* If Pozzo and
Godot can be viewed as images of a malevolent God then it
seems that this vision was derived from Marcion and his considerable influence.

APPENDIX B.
Political & Aesthetic Influence of Marcion

At about the same time that interest in the theology of Marcion was renewed, at the turn of the last century, the historical roots of Christianity were meticulously investigated with startling results. During the 1930s in Germany a dominant current of this speculation helped to provide justification for a church movement which attained the ultimate Gentile fantasy: a Jewless Christianity. European society was spiritually prepared to receive a new leader, a secularized Messiah in the form of Hitler. Large segments of this society came to believe that the Old and New Testaments were outmoded and that the future belonged to the third and final age of human development. In the early 1930s the third stage for the new political Messiah was set. Since the turn of the century a number of German-speaking intellectuals and writers — not a few of them Jews — had been considerably influenced by the doctrine of Marcion. In Germany the advocates for a radical rethinking of modern Christianity felt impelled to hasten the arrival of their Messiah by appealing to a peculiar though central theme in Christian apocalyptical messianism which gained widespread support among the German adherents of the new dispensation. The new League for a German Church not only aryanized Christian mythology but also paved the way for the religious acceptance of the Third Reich. Fritz Stern, in his cultural history of German ideology, has persuasively demonstrated how this basic notion in revolutionary Christian renewal found a tender spot in the hearts of Nazi supporters. See Fritz Stern, *The Politics of Cultural Despair: A Study in the Rise of the Germanic Ideology* (Berkeley: University of California Press, 1963); Norman Cohn, *The Pursuit of the Millenium* (London: Secker and Warburg, 1957), pp. 99-123; and Karl Löwith, *Meanings in History: The Theological Implications of the Philosophy of History* (Chicago: University of Chicago Press, 1949), pp. 145-59, 208-13. For the literary application of Joachimite prophecy, especially in D. H. Lawrence, see Philip Rieff, *The Triumph of the Therapeutic* (New York: Harper and Row, 1966), pp. 229-31. On the German church, see Arthur Cochrane, *The Church's Confession under Hitler* (Philadelphia: Westminster Press, 1962), p. 75. On the influence of Marcion, especially with regard to Kafka, see William Johnston, *The Austrian Mind* (Berkeley: University of California Press, 1972), pp. 271-72. See also Franz Kuna's perceptive comments on the appeal of Marcionism to the modern mind, *Kafka: Literature as Corrective Punishment* (Bloomington: Indiana University Press, 1974), pp. 45-46.

With Marcion in mind, the German churchmen and party faithful harked back to the messianic utopianism of Joachim de Floris, whose prophecies radicalized and animated Christian hope for a thorough renewal of dogma, faith, and commitment. In brief, this medieval mystic of the left wing of the church postulated that historical time was divided into three great parts, each corresponding dialectically to a successive stage in the evolution of the Trinity. In this scheme of things the Gods of the Old and New Testaments seemed deficient and outdated, and mankind (or at least its finest members) would only be redeemed through the advent of the Holy Ghost, who would gather up all true believers into an exclusive *ecclesia spiritualis,* into a third kingdom. In the minds of German Christians and National Socialist ideologues the Joachimite prophecy was transformed from idea to reality and neatly set in the context of German history and mythology. According to their reasoning the medieval and Wilhelmian Reichs would give way to the third and last Reich, led by a savior, a *novus dux,* Adolf Hitler. As far as they were concerned the cycle was complete. The awaited one had come at last. This spirit of ideas was also reflected in literature. In *Reading Finnegans Wake* (New York: Barnes and Noble, 1959) Frances Boldereff discusses, for example, the profound influence that Ibsen's play *The Emperor Julian* had upon Joyce. In this play Julian is made to say: "The Third Empire, the Messiah? Not the Jews' Messiah, but the Messiah of the two empires, the spirit and the world" (p. 198). And at the very end of *The Family Moskat,* the chronicle of a Polish Jewish family on the eve of Hitler's invasion, Isaac Bashevis Singer writes: "The Messiah will come soon. . . . Death is the Messiah. That's the real truth" (trans. A. H. Gross [New York: Noonday Press, 1950], p. 611).

Throughout much of his early career Hitler was considered by many to be a buffoon. Some thought him to be a charlatan, others a fool possessed by a devil. D'Annunzio saw him simply as a "ferocious clown." If enthusiasm is any measure of loyalty, the majority of his followers must have seen him as a projection of their own miserable selves, the portrait of the little man at last triumphant over the forces that conspire to keep him little. The intense identification that he inspired in his admirers was undoubtedly the secret of his success as a leader and manipulator of men. The new age of democracy, the emancipation of the masses, demanded a spokesman for the millions of small voices normally ignored in the dealings of the powerbrokers. Hitler, more than the others, fulfilled that need with a vengeance. If the interchange of clown and monster seems difficult to discern, particularly as reflected in *Waiting for Godot,* perhaps this horrific metamorphosis is more evident in a controversial film of Charlie Chaplin, *The Great Dictator.*

Like Beckett, Chaplin owes much to the commedia dell'
arte. And in his film Chaplin used two roles for one person.
He made Charlot (as the French call The Little Tramp) play
both Pierrot and Harlequin, the innocent and the demon.
Thus Andrew Sarris, the film critic, observes: "What, then,
is great about *The Great Dictator?* Simply the remarkable
duality of Chaplin as the Dictator and the Barber. Not simply as one or the other, but as both in one.... They inhabit
each other somehow as Chaplin and Hitler inhabited each
other" (*Confessions of a Cultist: On the Cinema 1955/1969*
[New York: Simon and Schuster, 1970], p. 127). Regarding
this film another comment of Sarris can also be applied to
Beckett's play and perhaps explain its initial failure before
the general American audience: "Within moments Chaplin
can glide from the ridiculous to the sublime and back to the
ridiculous. This talent for the tragicomic is seldom appreciated in America. You're either funny or you're serious and
that's that"(p. 126).

It is obvious that Charlot as the little barber is different
from Hitler the dictator just as Gogo the tramp is different
from Pozzo the slavemaster. But during the thirties Chaplin
must have sensed the uncanny connection, a certain similarity
between his brand of clownery and Hitler's public image.
After viewing films of Hitler, Chaplin thought him to be
a bad imitation of Charlot, but not bad enough to keep
the actor from doing an imitation of Hitler himself. Their
politics, of course, were radically opposed, but the mustache,
the appeal, were the same to the little man in the street.

In 1937 it was suggested that Chaplin make this film sati-
rizing Hitler in which he would have a double role. The film
that appeared in 1940, *The Great Dictator,* was an uncanny,
eerie metamorphosis of doubles, an exchange of roles between the gentle Pierrot and the blustering Harlequin.
Chaplin played the part of a Jewish barber who through
mistaken identities somehow assumes the role of the German

dictator to whom he bears an exact resemblance. Despite
the film's popular success, the critical reviews found it hard
to accept the dramatic propriety of the celebrated final speech
where the barber, mistaken for Hitler and standing in his
place, pleads passionately for brotherhood and world peace
before a gigantic Nazi party rally.

Here Chaplin the clown stepped out of the role, briefly,
to speak as Chaplin the humanitarian, to preach directly to
the audience, to the flabby conscience of Western civilization.
(One recalls the less emphatic interruptions of Didi who turns
to the audience and calls it "that bog," that same fetid marsh-
land of the West which Rimbaud referred to in the course of
his wanderings through Africa.) What was objectionable to the
critics was the expression of Chaplin's personal views in so direct a manner, in an oratorical delivery that interrupted the
narrative flow of the film. This was a common device in the
commedia dell'arte, and Beckett used the same technique,
though more subtly, to remind his audience that it is behold-
ing a play, that this work is deliberately self-conscious, in
order to suggest that there is something else of import beyond the boundaries delimited by the stage. Chaplin's appeal
was not lost on his audience. There he stood, the pathetic,
fantastic figure of a Jewish barber, quoting Luke and pleading
for tolerance through the mouth of Hitler. For a discussion
of Chaplin's film as drama, see Eric Bentley, *The Life of the
Drama* (New York: Atheneum, 1974), pp. 346-47. Concerning
the major shift in the evolution of the modern theater and
film, Jean Renoir writes: "This question of exterior and inte-
rior truth is at the heart of the acting profession. In the nineteenth century the bourgeois intellectual drama reached its
peak. We are now in the process of emerging from that trend
and the *commedia dell'arte* is coming back with a rush" (*My
Life and My Films* [New York: Atheneum, 1974], p. 159).
Both Beckett and Chaplin have capitalized on this development.

Some time after making the film Chaplin admitted that had he been fully aware of his subject's true character, he would not have attempted to present Hitler in so frivolous a light. For Chaplin and many others Hitler was not the creature they thought they saw. Chaplin tried to limit his interpretation of Hitler to that of a sixteenth-century Harlequin, a bumbling, misguided, ill-tempered mountebank. As history quickly bore out, the image later appreciated of Hitler was more akin to that of the first Harlequin, Herla the Erlkonig, a king of hell, leading his torch-bearing troupe across Europe during the Dark Ages. Those who observed Hitler's spectacular rallies — the writer Charles Fair, for example — were struck by the primitive atmosphere of awe and terror: "One seemed, for an instant, to be back in the wilderness of ancient Europe, surrounded by strange night cries and movements in the darkness" (*From the Jaws of Victory* [New York: Simon and Schuster, 1971], p. 349). Europe had finally cast off its Judeo-Christian heritage and returned to its barbarian past. The legacy of this barbarism had never really vanished down through the centuries, but during the years between the wars fascism unabashedly threw off the fetters that kept brutality in check. Fascists were proud to proclaim their pagan heritage openly. The Jewish God had been overthrown and a secularized Messiah of sorts installed in his place. The dreams of Marcion and Joachim finally bore fruit. The third kingdom had been established, one which all concerned, after the fact, would wish had never been realized. This is the same nightmare with which Didi is struggling in his waiting for Godot. He wants him to come but he has a dim premonition that he will be sorry to see him appear.

This same play of politics and secularized theology also has its place on the Left. Isaac Deutscher gives testimony to the relevance of Beckett's play to the political climate of Russia. Hopeful that the Soviet experiment might one day attain fulfillment, once cleansed of Stalinism, Deutscher described the present state of affairs there as akin to "the mood of *Waiting for Godot*" (*The Unfinished Revolution* [Oxford: Oxford University Press, 1967], p. 100). Indeed it would be unfair to limit the image of the demonic secular Messiah to National Socialism. Friedrich Heer has traced its somewhat more modest development in international socialism: "The Leftist social revolutionary Invanov-Rasumnik compared the Revolution, in *Russia and Ionia* (1920), to the birth of Jesus of Bethlehem. A sect calling itself 'New Testament' endowed Lenin, as bearer of the 'Third Testament with the redemptive power received by the Fraticelli followers of Joachim of Flora" (*Europe, Mother of Revolutions* [New York: Praeger, 1972], p. 346). On the political implications of *Waiting for Godot*, see Eric Bentley, *The Theater of Commitment* (New York: Atheneum, 1967), p. 203. It has been remarked that Beckett's work exhibits few direct political or historical references; however, Bernard Lalande and others have concluded that Beckett was not insensitive to contemporary history as it unfolded around him and must have incorporated some of its elements into his drama (Lalande, *"En Attendant Godot": Beckett* [Paris: Hatier, 1970], p. 23).

NOTES

Chapter 1

1. John Gruen, "Samuel Beckett Talks about Beckett," *Vogue,* London ed., 28 (February 1970):108.
2. John Pilling, *Samuel Beckett* (London: Routledge & Kegan Paul, 1976), p. 18.
3. Hugh Kenner, "Writers' Writers," *New York Times Book Review,* December 4, 1977, p. 58.
4. Alan Schneider, "Waiting for Beckett — A Personal Chronicle," *Chelsea Review* 14, no. 2 (Autumn 1958):3-20.
5. On the function of portmanteau words see Lewis Carroll, *The Hunting of the Snark* (New York: Branhall, 1962), p. 34; and Robert Sutherland, *Language and Lewis Carroll* (The Hague: Mouton, 1970), p. 152.
6. Alec Reid, "From Beginning to Date," in *Samuel Beckett,* ed. Ruby Cohn (New York: McGraw-Hill, 1975), p. 64.
7. Alain Robbe-Grillet, *For a New Novel,* trans. Richard Howard (New York: Grove Press, 1965), p. 120.
8. Martin Esslin, *The Theater of the Absurd* (New York: Anchor Books, 1969), p. 44.
9. Samuel Beckett, "Dante . . . Bruno. Vico . . Joyce," in *Our Exagmination Round His Factification for Incamination of Work in Progress* (London: Faber & Faber, 1961), p. 14. Unless stated otherwise, in this book all references to *Godot* are taken from these editions: *En attendant Godot* (Paris: Editions de Minuit, 1952) and *Waiting for Godot* (New York: Grove Press, 1954).
10. Samuel Beckett, *Malone Dies* (New York: Grove Press, 1965), p. 192.
11. Samuel Beckett, *Watt* (New York: Grove Press, 1970), p. 77.
12. A. J. Leventhal, "The Beckett Hero," in *Samuel Beckett,* ed. Martin Esslin (New York: Prentice-Hall, 1965), p. 40.
13. I have also tried to follow Patrick Murray's wise counsel on

this matter: "There is every sign that Beckett, like his mentor Joyce, derives a malicious pleasure from contriving just such puzzles as will set literary detectives to work. Then, having inspected the results of their activities, he affects an attitude of pained surprise at what they have to report" (*Samuel Beckett* [Cork: Mercier Press, 1970], p. 104). For all his mischievousness, I believe that Beckett, through constant return to certain symbols and themes, is trying to put forth a particular notion about dramatic development, one that is consistent with his stance of deliberate obfuscation.

14. Samuel Beckett, *Molloy* (New York: Grove Press, 1970), p. 41.

15. On this linguistic theme see Michel Pierssens, *La Tour de Babil* (Paris: Editions de Minuit, 1976); p. 122; and Louis Wolfson, *Le Schizo et les langues* (Paris: Gallimard, 1970), p. 11. See also Betty Rojtman, *Forme et signification dans le théâtre de Beckett* (Paris: Nizet, 1976); and Fernande Saint-Martin, *Samuel Beckett et l'univers de la fiction* (Montréal: Les Presses de l'université de Montréal, 1976).

16. See Roland Barthes, *S/Z* (Paris: Seuil, 1970), and *Le Plaisir du texte* (Paris: Seuil, 1973).

17. Vivian Mercier, *Beckett/Beckett* (New York: Oxford University Press, 1977), p. vii.

18. Melvin J. Friedman, ed. *Samuel Beckett Now* (Chicago: Chicago University Press, 1970), p. 26.

19. Quoted by Deirdre Bair, *Samuel Beckett: A Biography* (New York: Harcourt Brace Jovanovich, 1978), p. 403.

Chapter 2

1. Paul Jennings, "Making Them Laugh," *Saturday Book*, no. 31 (1971):54.

The clowns of Beckett and Cervantes have their origins in the early Italian comic tradition. Names betray functions and so it is with all the characters of the commedia dell'arte, especially its most famous son, Harlequin, who seems to be a distant ancestor of Pozzo. Enid Welsford writes that "Harlequin has a mixed ancestry, and is himself an odd hybrid creature, in part devil, created by popular fancy, in part wandering mountebank from Italy" (*The Fool: His Social and Literary History* [New York: Anchor, 1961], p. 293). In Italy Dante mentions a minor demon, Alichino, who was accompanied by another one named Draghignazzo, which means "great dragon." Whether Harlequin first appeared in northern or southern Europe, he can be traced back to a medieval troupe that wandered through England and France and was notorious as the *maisnie Herlechin* in the twelfth century. This group was mainly recalled for staging a terrifying night procession called "the Wild Hunt," which seems to have been reminiscent of the demonic pre-Christian rituals and practices abolished by the official religion. By the thirteenth century Harlequin makes his first theatrical appearance in Adam le Bossu's play, *Le Jeu de la feuillée.* Here his bearing seems to have lost some of its more frightening features even though he remains in this play a king of demons. Curiously enough, in this work he does not appear in person; he sends instead his little messenger, Croquesot, to announce his nonarrivals. See Normand Cartier, *Le Bossu désenchanté* (Geneva: Droz, 1971).

It seems likely that Beckett's genius was able to combine these features of Harlequin's evolution — the demonic and the comic — in his two pairs of clowns. In the course of his development as a comic type Harlequin gradually became associated with another figure, Bertoldo — like himself a valet but of a slightly inferior status. Bertoldo typified the rustic mentality. As a wily peasant his rough exterior often concealed an acute folk wisdom. Together Harlequin and Bertoldo formed a comic pair, the most famous and durable among several that would find their richest expression in the improvisational theater of the *commedia dell'arte,* which swept Europe in the sixteenth century. It is from this pair of buffoons that Beckett and Cervantes ultimately derived their own clowns. See also Giulio Cesare Croce, *Bertoldo, Bertoldino, e Cacasenno* (Milan: Feltrinelli, 1965); Cyril Beaumont, *The History of Harlequin* (New York: Blom, 1967); Pierre Louis Duchartre, *The Italian Comedy* (London: Harrap, 1929); Allardyce Nicoll, *The World of Harlequin* (Cambridge: Cambridge University Press, 1963), and Giacomo Oreglia, *The Commedia dell' Arte* (New York: Hill and Wang, 1968).

3. John Moore, "A Farewell to Something," *Tulane Drama Review* 5 (September 1960): 59. See also Christine Brooke-Rose, "Samuel Beckett and the Anti-Novel," *London Magazine* 5 (December 1958): 38-46; John Fletcher, "Beckett and the Fictional Tradition,"*Annales* (publiées par la Faculté des Lettres et Sciences Humaines de Toulouse) 1 (1965):147-58; and John Pilling, *Samuel Beckett* (London: Routledge & Kegan Paul, 1976), p. 38.

4. Lukacs, writing on Cervantes, touches on a common theme that links him to Beckett: "Thus the first great novel of world literature stands at the beginning of the time when the Christian God began to foresake the world; when man became lonely and could find meaning and substance only in his own soul, whose home was nowhere" (Georg

Lukacs, *The Theory of the Novel* [Cambridge: M.I.T. Press, 1971],
p. 103).

5. See Ihab Hassan, *The Literature of Silence* (New York: Knopf,
1967), pp. 111-200.

6. Hugh Kenner, *Flaubert, Joyce, and Beckett* (Boston: Beacon,
1962), p. 70. With reference to Beckett, Gabriel Vahanian observes:
"The whole play is constructed around the irrelevance of Christian
concepts and especially around the nonsensical or Quixotic quality
of Christian existence" (*The Death of God* [New York: Braziller,
1961], p. 120). A curious footnote in the history of literature: in
1843 Sören Kierkegaard wrote a review of A. E. Scribe's play, *The
First Love,* the two main characters of which are named Charles and
Emmeline. In this essay he notes that "it is altogether remarkable that
the whole of European literature lacks a feminine counterpart to Don
Quixote. May not the time for this be coming. . . ?" (*Either/Or* [Prince-
ton, N. J.: Princeton University Press, 1944), 2:255. Kierkegaard seems
to be unaware that such a work was written by a British author, Sophie
Lennox, in 1773. In any event six years after Kierkegaard's observation
Flaubert would begin to fulfill this task anew.

7. See Albert Thibaudet, *Le Liseur des romans* (Paris: Gallimard,
1925), p. xv.

8. Erich Auerbach, *Mimesis* (New York: Anchor, 1957), p. 311.

9. Américo Castro, *Hacia Cervantes* (Madrid: Taurus, 1967), pp. 477-
85. See also J. Chaix-Ruy, "Cervantes, Flaubert, et Pirandello," *Anales
Cervantinos* 6 (1957): 123-32.

10. Concerning Don Quixote's conflict over reality and illusion see
Richard Predmore, *The World of Don Quixote* (Cambridge, Mass.:
Harvard University Press, 1967), pp. 53-97. On the same theme in
Beckett see Raymond Federman, "Beckettian Paradox," in *Samuel
Beckett Now,* ed. Melvin J. Friedman, pp. 103-17.

11. See August Closs, "Formprobleme und Möglichkeiten zur
Gestaltung der Tragödie in der Gegenwart," *Stil- und Formprobleme*
5 (1960): 483-91; and Renato Oliva, *Samuel Beckett,* (Milan: Mursia,
1967), pp. 61-72.

12. See Nicoll, *World of Harlequin,* p. 167. See also A. Pellizari,
"Saggio de uno studio sulle relazioni del Cervantes con l'Italia,"
Rassegna 9 (1916):319.

13. See Kay Dick, *Pierrot* (London: Hutchinson, 1960), p. 41.
On the influence of the *commedia* tradition in modern literature,
see Martin Green, *Children of the Sun: A Narrative of Decadence
in England after 1918* (New York: Basic Books, 1976), with particular

reference to Carlo Gozzi and Nancy Cunard, pp. 22-23, 32, 249.

14. Dick, *Pierrot,* p. 95.

15. Allardyce Nicoll reproduces a revealing print of Harlequin, dating from Cervantes's time, which depicts him mounted, wearing decrepit armor with a pot on his head for a helmet, carrying a lance, going off to uphold the beauty and name of his mistress before the entire world — a portrait quite like that of Don Quixote himself. See *World of Harlequin,* p. 168.

16. See Hugh Kenner, *Samuel Beckett* (Berkeley: University of California Press, 1968), p. 67; and Harold Clurman, *Lies like Truth* (New York: Macmillan, 1958), pp. 220-25.

17. See W. S. Hendrix, "Sancho Panza and the Comic Types of the Sixteenth Century," *Homenaje ofrecido a Menéndez Pidal* (Madrid: Hernando, 1925), 2:485-94; and Francisco Márquez Villanueva, "Sobre la génesis literaria de Sancho Panza," *Anales Cervantinos* 2 (1958): 123-55.

18. W. W. Skeat, *Etymological Dictionary of the English Language* (Oxford: Clarendon Press, 1910), p. 630. See also *Culpeper's Complete Herbal* (London: Foulsham, n.d.), p. 363.

19. Leo Spitzer, *Linguistics and Literary History* (Princeton, N. J.: Princeton University Press, 1948), p. 49. With reference to the meaning of names it should be noted in passing that the most celebrated Italian commedia actor in Spain bore the name Ganassa. Since different performers in this theatrical tradition had to take distinctive names, this clown's designation is all the more intriguing, for Ganassa is the northern Italian dialect form of the word *ganascia* which means "jaw." In its French form, *ganache,* it suggests someone who talks too much for his own good. During his travels throughout Europe Ganassa held the honor of being the first actor on record to play the role of Harlequin. Such observations tend to support the hypothesis that Don Quixote was in part based on the character of Harlequin. See my *"Waiting for Godot: A Modern Don Quixote?" Hispania* 57 (Dec. 1974):876-85 and "Cervantes's Use of Character Names and the *Commedia dell'Arte,"* *Romance Notes* 17, no. 3 (Spring 1977): 314-19.

20. See Martín de Riquer, *Aproximación al Quijote* (Barcelona: Teide, 1976), pp. 82-83.

21. Constantino Láscaris Comneno, "El Nombre de Don Quijote," *Anales Cervantinos* 2 (1952): 364.

22. Ruby Cohn, *Samuel Beckett: The Comic Gamut* (New Brunswick, N. J.: Rutgers University Press, 1962), p. 213. See also her *Back to Beckett* (Princeton, N. J.: Princeton University Press, 1973), pp. 127-39.

23. Marquez Villanueva, "Sobre la genesis literaria de Sancho Panz," p. 155. References to *Don Quixote* are from the translation by J. M. Cohen (Baltimore, Md.: Penguin Books, 1970).

24. Spitzer, *Linguistics and Literary History,* p. 45.

25. Predmore, *World of Don Quixote,* pp. 84-85.

26. In an illuminating chapter, "The Dragon and the Hero," Esther Harding traces the origin of the wandering knight back to the earliest legends concerning Saint George, whose traditional shrine is found in Al-Khudr, the Palestinian village bearing his name, and whose feast day is April 26: "The latter day is called 'the feast of spring, which makes everything green:' Al-Khudr means 'the Green One' or 'the Ever Living One.' This saint, under the name either of George or Al-Khudr, was believed to have peculiar powers — in particular, power to heal lunatics. The procedure prescribed to bring about a cure was as follows: At the time of the saint's feast, the sick person was brought to the shrine and a lamb was offered in sacrifice. The sick man was then shut into a dark cavern at the back of the shrine, where he spent the night alone" *(Psychic Energy* [New York: Pantheon, 1963], p. 254). This passage closely follows in its details Don Quixote's encounter with the Knight of the Green Coat, shortly after which he descends into the cave of Montesinos. Whether Cervantes was or was not familiar with the early Christian legend, the importance of the story lies in what Harding describes as the hero's confrontation with the dragon viewed as the destructive side of himself. In Jungian terms, the hero and dragon may be one and the same creature. In varying degrees Sancho and Estragon fulfill this function in that they lead their companions to a higher awareness of themselves and reality.

27. See John Sheedy, "The Net," in his *Casebook on "Waiting for Godot"* (New York: Grove Press, 1967), pp. 159-66.

28. Salvador de Madariaga, *Don Quixote* (London: Oxford University Press, 1961), pp. 137-56. See also René Girard, *Mensonge romantique et vérité romanesque* (Paris: Grasset, 1961), pp. 145-57.

29. Cohn, *Samuel Beckett,* p. 214.

30. Thomas Mann comments perceptively on this Christian aspect of brutality: "In no other place comes out so strongly as here [Cervantes's] utter readiness to exalt and to abase his hero. But abasement and exaltation are a twin conception the essence of which is distinctly Christian. Their psychological union, their marriage in a comic medium, shows how very much Don Quixote is a product of Christian culture, Christian doctrine, and Christian humanity" ("Voyage with Don Quixote," in *Essays of Three Decades,*

trans. H. T. Lowe-Porter [New York: Knopf, 1947], p. 453.

31. Madariaga, *Don Quixote*, p. 121.

32. Miguel de Unamuno, referring to Cervantes's classic, anticipates Vladimir's anguish on this score: "There is no future; there never is a future. What they call the future is one of the greatest lies. The real future is today" (*La Vida de Don Quijote* [Madrid: Aguilar, 1966], 2:73.

33. In this context, Kafka's parable on Sancho Panza is worth considering. In it Kafka expresses the belief that Sancho, ironically, exorcises his demon, named Don Quixote, and for the sake of responsibility, follows him about on his crusades. See Franz Kafka, "The Truth about Sancho Panza," in *The Complete Stories*, trans. Willa and Edwin Muir (New York: Schocken, 1971), p. 430.

34. In a penetrating essay Edith Kern likens the mood of *Waiting for Godot* to that of the *commedia dell'arte*. Elements of the grotesque, contempt for literacy, and a fondness for the stage business of low comedy combine to link Beckett and the Italian tradition. Kern, however, feels that Beckett's play lacks the commedia's most notable feature, "its improvisation or its stock characters in their traditional orchestration" ("Beckett and the Spirit of the Commedia dell'Arte," *Modern Drama* 9 [December 1966]:260); see also John Fletcher, *Forces in Modern French Drama* [New York: Ungar, 1972]), p. 203. A closer look at the textual differences between the French and English versions will show that Beckett is quite flexible and prepared to adapt his work to various audiences. While the characters do not appear wearing traditional commedia costumes, both comic pairs are faithful to the outlines of the evolving relationships between Harlequin and Pierrot. Beckett's tramps spend most of their lives improvising and making pratfalls and skits to help them pass the time. Kern also mentions, in passing, various performances of plays-within-the-play, and this feature of Beckett's stagecraft, if explored in depth and from different angles, should add more dimensions to the understanding of the drama.

Beckett, though born after the turn of the twentieth century, seems to have been influenced by the previous one. According to Jean-Bertrand Barrère, "Victor Hugo took the characters of the Commedia dell'Arte as examples of embodiments of the grotesque" ("Victor Hugo's interest in the grotesque in his poetry and drawings," in *French 19th Century Painting and Literature*, ed. Ulrich Finke [New York: Harper & Row, 1972], pp. 258-59). Barrère goes on to remark that Hugo in his first novels combined these grotesque comic figures with depictions of characters based on Don Quixote and Sancho Panza.

And by way of conclusion Barrère is struck by Hugo's use of such imagery to such a degree that certain lines evoke the "symbol of the *condition humaine* which already was so akin to Beckett's beggar (Lucky), permanently enslaved to some Pozzo" (p. 277). Beckett's clowns are dressed in the costumes of music hall comedians, and the author's preference for silent comedy films was demonstrated by his collaboration with Buster Keaton on his own attempts with film.

35. David Madden, *Harlequin's Stick — Charlie's Cane* (Bowling Green, Ohio: Popular Press, 1975), p. 150. For a recent study on Cervantes's use of consciousness, see Robert Alter, "The Mirror of Knighthood and the World of Mirrors," *Partial Magic: The Novel as a Self-Conscious Genre* (Berkeley: University of California Press, 1975), pp. 1-29. See also Marthe Robert, *The Old and the New: From Don Quixote to Kafka,* trans. Carol Cosman (Berkeley: University of California Press, 1977).

Chapter 3

1. Renée Riese Hubert, "The Couple and the Performance in Samuel Beckett's Plays," *L'Esprit Créateur* 2 (Winter 1962): 177.

2. Katharine Worth, *Beckett the Shape Changer* (London: Routledge & Kegan Paul, 1975), p. 11.

3. See Ralph Tymms, *Doubles in Literary Psychology* (Cambridge: Bowes & Bowes, 1949), p. 15.

4. In a more thorough work on this subject Robert Rogers believes that Tymm's judgment holds true for what Rogers terms manifest as opposed to latent doubling. *Waiting for Godot* deals precisely with doubling on the latent level, and this only becomes evident through examination of the play's inner structure. See Robert Rogers, *The Double in Literature* (Detroit, Mich.: Wayne State University Press, 1970), p. 31.

5. It should be recalled that in *Hamlet* accuser and guilty, hunter and hunted, confront one another through a fog of antipathy and recrimination. Here Shakespeare offered a parallelism between the traveling players' performance and the details of Claudius's evil-doing, and he offered it twice just as Beckett would do in his play. When he speaks to the players, Hamlet specifies "the purpose of the playing, whose end, both at the first and now, was and is, to hold, as 'twere, the mirror up to nature." The pantomime and playlet serve as reflections of unbearable reality and of unutterable truth.

If this episode is the central scene of *Hamlet,* it must also serve ends beyond merely informing the pit of the king's guilt. At this critical juncture of the drama, critic Eleanor Prosser observes about Hamlet: "His hatred of Claudius is so intense that he is led subconsciously to identify himself with the murderer" (*Hamlet and Revenge* [London: Oxford University Press, 1967], p. 179). The scene to which Prosser refers has the triple function of informing the king, the audience, and last, though less obviously, Hamlet himself of the dark web of the crime. True to his equivocal nature, Hamlet does not clearly perceive the ultimate reality that the contrived playlet has provoked. He approaches the truth — the awareness of his psychological involvement in his father's death — but at the same time he remains just this side of complete recognition of his state of mind. The dumb show and the play-within-the-play allow him a glimpse of reality, a glance into the mirror held up to nature, but for the briefest of moments. Beckett uses the same two dramatic devices in *Godot* to convey the theme of nonrecognition of reality. For additional critical comparison of these two plays see Bert O. States, *The Shape of Paradox: An Essay on "Waiting for Godot"* (Berkeley: University of California Press, 1978), pp. 86-87. See also Lee Sheridan Cox, *Figurative Design in Hamlet: The Significance of the Dumb Show* (Columbus: Ohio State University Press, 1973); and Kemp Malone, "Etymologies for *Hamlet*," *Studies in Heroic Legend and in Current Speech* (Copenhagen: Rosenkilde and Bagger, 1959), pp. 204-25. For the influence of Shakespeare on Beckett, see Ruby Cohn, *Modern Shakespeare Offshoots* (Princeton University Press, 1976), pp. 375-88. See also Avi Erlich, *Hamlet's Absent Father* (Princeton, N. J.: Princeton University Press, 1977).

6. See David Grossvogel, *The Blasphemers: The Theater of Brecht, Ionesco, Beckett, Genet* (Ithaca, N. Y.: Cornell University Press, 1966), p. 85. See also Guy Croussy, *Beckett* (Paris: Hachette, 1971), p. 116.

7. This concept of play has been explored by Johan Huizinga in his *Homo Ludens* (New York: Roy Publishers, 1950), p. 78.

8. Sigmund Freud, *Jokes and Their Relation to the Unconscious*, trans. James Strachey (New York: Norton, 1960).

9. See Louis Perche, *Beckett* (Paris: Editions du Centurion, 1969), p. 91.

10. Marthe Robert, *The Old and the New*, p. 27. See also Wolfgang Wickler, *Mimicry in Plants and Animals* (New York: McGraw-Hill, 1974).

11. Alain Robbe-Grillet, *For a New Novel*, p. 120. For a detailed treatment of this theatrical technique used by Beckett to dramatize character growth and development, see Robert Nelson, *Play within*

a Play: The Dramatist's Conception of His Art (New Haven, Conn.: Yale University Press, 1958).

12. Martin Esslin, *Theater of the Absurd,* p. 29. On the relationship of Joyce and Beckett, see Deirdre Bair, *Samuel Beckett,* pp. 67-85.

13. Lionel Abel, *Metatheatre: A New View of Dramatic Form* (New York: Hill and Wang, 1963), p. 134.

14. Adaline Glasheen, *A Second Census of Finnegans Wake* (Evanston, Ill.: Northwestern University Press, 1963), p. 25. Here is the passage in which the reference is to be found: "You is feeling like you was lost in the bush, boy? You says: It is a puling sample jungle of woods. You most shouts out: Bethicket me for a stump of a beech if I have the poultriest notions what the farest he all means" (James Joyce, *Finnegans Wake* [New York: Viking, 1939], p. 112.

15. On the aesthetic relationship between these two writers, see my "Joycean Echoes in *Waiting for Godot,*" *Research Studies* 43 (June 1975):71-87; and "Naming Day in No-Man's Land: Beckett's Use of Names in *Waiting for Godot,*" *Boston University Journal* 22 (Winter 1974): 20-29.

16. Joyce, *Finnegans Wake,* p. 467. Commenting on Beckett's work, Vivian Mercier writes: "The play as a whole radiates the same kind of patient, mocking Pyrrhonism as *Finnegans Wake*" ("A Pyrrhonian Eclogue," *Hudson Review* 7 [Winter 1955]: 621.

17. G. C. Barnard, *Samuel Beckett, A New Approach: A Study of the Novels and Plays* (New York: Dodd, Mead, 1970).

18. Samuel Beckett, "Dante. . .Bruno.Vico. .Joyce," in *Our Exagmination,* pp. 3-22.

19. William York Tindall, *A Reader's Guide to Finnegans Wake* (New York: Farrar, Straus & Giroux, 1969), p. 42.

20. Mercier, "Pyrrhonian Eclogue," p. 624.

21. Joyce, too, uses the routine of the shoe exchange in similar circumstances where he writes, for example, in the *Wake:* "Mr R. E. Meehan is in misery in his billyboots" (p. 466). Characteristically, a common Irish name is employed here to evoke the basic conflict of Zoroastrian religion, which is the cosmic confrontation between Ormazd and Ahriman, the gods of good and evil, light and darkness. Again one reads: "The misery billyboots I used to lend him before we split and, be the hole in the year, they were laking like heaven's reflexes" (p. 467). This line is to be found on the same page with the previously mentioned possible allusion to Beckett in the *Wake.* And whatever the significance of this reference to "Sam," it may have caught Sam Beckett's eye and provided food for thought. The shoe exchange,

the enigmatic manifestations of divine judgment, the eternal clash of good and evil, all these alternating experiences underscore the uncertainty rooted in human expectations and divine providence.

22. There is a minor tradition in Christian painting in which the image of the pig is used in the company of a suffering saint: "Saint Anthony was said to have been originally a swineherd, and is therefore ordinarily represented as accompanied by a hog. In Pisano's picture in the National Gallery of 'Saint Anthony and Saint George,' the two saints confront each other, and at the feet of one is the pig and of the other the vanquished dragon. Amongst the figures carved in Henry the Seventh Chapel at Westminster will be found St. Anthony, a bearded figure in frock and scapular, and at his side a giant pig is standing" (F. Edward Hulme, *Symbolism in Christian Art* [London: Macmillan, 1891], p. 180). In Christian iconography the pig is usually intended to signify insult and revilement. The Romans used it to deprecate the ancient Jews, and as a sign of abuse the Christians continued this custom. E. P. Stevens writes: "Henry VIII showed his contempt of the Roman See by using for official purposes a paper with a water-mark of a hog wearing a tiara, just as the Republican parliament substituted a fool's cap and bells for the king's arms on the official paper of the realm" (*Animal Symbolism in Ecclesiastical Architecture* [London: Heineman, 1896], p. 195). Lucky's name shares other linguistically bestial resonances. To return to the symbol of the calf, it is curious to note that in Irish this word is *laogh*, which is pronounced "lekh," and the word *luighein* signifies "two cloven feet as of a cow." See Fr. Allan McDonald, *Gaelic Words and Expressions from South Uist and Eriskey* (Dublin: Dublin Institute for Advanced Studies, 1958), p. 169. In reference to Gaelic it is worth noting that in Celtic mythology the sun god is known as Lugh. From this perspective Lucky could be seen as a grotesque form of Apollo who is opposed by Pozzo as a low form of Dionysus or Bacchus. Sighle Kennedy has pointed out that in Greek *lykos* signifies "wolf," and the expression "to see a wolf" means "to be struck dumb." Apart from his celebrated monologue Lucky remains dumb throughout the play. In its Latin derivatives the word "wolf" is related to "convulse" and "revulsion" which also describe Lucky's state. See Stephen Potter and Laurens Sargent, *Pedigree: The Origins of Words from Nature* (New York: Taplinger, 1973), p. 65. Meillet observes that "le loup ayant un fort machoîre, *Lupus, lupatus* ont désigné des objects en forme de dents de loup" *Dictionnaire etymologique de la langue latine,* 2d ed. (Paris: Klincksieck, 1959), p. 370. See also Carl Darling Buck, *A Dictionary of Selected Synonyms*

in the Principal Indo-European Languages: A Contribution to the History of Ideas (Chicago: University of Chicago Press, 1965), p. 185.

23. According to Joyce, the Ondt with his "chairmanlooking" smile is the incarnation of matter, space, and brute force. Shem as the Grace-hoper is not only "the sillybilly horing after ladybirdies" but the artist tormented by "His Gross the Ondt, prostrandvorous upon his dhrone, in his Papylonian babooshkies, smolking a special brunt of Hosana cigals, with unshrinkables farfalling from his unthinkables" (*Finnegans Wake*, p. 417). Here Joyce presents the philistine as the papist antichrist, the devil himself stoking the flames of eternal damnation on the body of the gracehoper.

24. Samuel Beckett, *Nouvelles et textes pour rien* (Paris: Editions de Minuit, 1958), p. 161. See also *Stories and Texts for Nothing,* (New York: Grove Press, 1967).

25. *The Oxford Classical Dictionary,* ed. N. G. L. Hammond and H. H. Scullard, 2d ed., (Oxford: Clarendon Press, 1970), p. 773.

26. A. Walton Litz, *The Art of James Joyce* (New York: Oxford University Press, 1964), p. 106.

27. *The Oxford English Dictionary* gives a few interesting examples of the word "knock" which tend to support this interpretation: "(Addison 1711) The Knight goes off... seeks all opportunities of being knock'd on the head," and also "(Barham 1840) To lie snoring there when your brethren are being knocked at head." On the central significance of place-names used by Beckett see Lawrence Harvey, *Samuel Beckett, Poet and Critic* (Princeton, N. J.: Princeton University Press, 1970), p. 150. On Beckett's word "knook," see also Colin Duckworth, *Angels of Darkness* (London: Barnes and Noble, 1972), pp. 67-68.

28. G. C. Barnard, *Samuel Beckett,* p. 95. See also R. Poulet, *La Lanterne magique* (Paris: Nouvelle Edition Debresse, 1956), pp. 236-42.

29. Another indirect reference to Shakespeare occurs only in the English version of *Waiting for Godot.* Twice Beckett mentions "the light of labours lost," an obvious nod toward *Love's Labour's Lost.* But why these two plays? *Love's Labour's Lost* is reckoned among Shakespeare's earliest and until recently least-appreciated dramas. *The Tempest,* on the other hand, is held to be his last play and one of the most popular. What critics used to dislike in the early play was the use of rather low comedy and fanciful elements, attributed to the commedia dell'arte. Only recently have similar sources been attributed to the more popular last play. Standing as markers of the beginning and the end of Shakespeare's career, they owe much to the

world of Italian low comedy. Beckett may have chosen them to emphasize again the notions of united opposites and merging contraries in
the realm of literary creativeness. By the use of similar sources and
theatrical devices Shakespeare created two entirely different atmo-
spheres, and likewise in Joyce the same elements are also present and
account for one of the principal sources of *Finnegans Wake*. Lucky's
speech as a mixture of high and low dramatic form produces an identical effect. See David Young, *The Heart's Forest: A Study of
Shakespeare's Pastoral Plays* (New Haven, Conn.: Yale University
Press, 1972), pp. 149-53. Beckett first refers to Miranda in his essay
on Proust: "Unlike Miranda he suffers with her whom he had not
seen suffer" (*Proust* [London: Chatto and Windus, 1931], p. 30).
See also M. C. Bradbrook, *Literature in Action* (New York: Barnes
and Noble, 1972), p. 30. The spirit of the commedia is equally present
in Joyce, according to Bernard Benstock, *Joyce-Again's Wake: An
Analysis of Finnegans Wake* (Seattle: University of Washington Press,
1965), pp. 35-36: "The strong element of pantomime which . . . dom-
inated much of Joyce's thinking in his conception of the *Wake,* is
equally linguistic. His Harlequins and Columbines wear their splashed
profusion of colors in a tumble of linguistic patterns of 'rudd yellan
gruebleen. . .' Actually the pantomime is never *seen* in *Finnegans
Wake;* it is there primarily because Joyce alludes to it" (pp. 108-9).
    30. G. C. Barnard, *Samuel Beckett,* p. 95.
    31. The rest of this passage deserves comment: ". . . matrimonial
gift of Matthew Dillon: a dwarf tree of glacial arborescence under
a transparent bellshade, matrimonial gift of Luke and Caroline Doyle:
an embalmed owl, matrimonial gift of Alderman John Hooper." Here
all divine endeavors have ceased. Three of the four evangelists have
brought gifts that remain frozen in an eerie immobility: Matthew's
clock, which heralded the chronology and time of the new dispensation,
no longer functions; Luke, who dwelt upon the crucifixion, brought
a stunted tree in mocking contrast to the glory of Christ's redemptive
death; John's owl, symbol of knowledge and wisdom, is mummified.
    32. William York Tindall, *A Reader's Guide to Finnegans Wake,*
p. 43.
    33. William York Tindall, "James Joyce and the Hermetic Tradition,"
Journal of the History of Ideas 15 (January 1954): 54. For a detailed
discussion of related themes, particularly the artist and his double, see
Hélène Cixous, *L'Exil de James Joyce ou l'art du remplacement* (Paris:
Grasset, 1968).
    34. For a thorough study of Joachim de Floris see Marjorie Reeves,

The Influence of Prophecy in the Later Middle Ages: A Study of Joachism (Oxford: Oxford University Press, 1969). On this major theme in Beckett's play Rolf Breuer writes: "Dabei kann man noch einmal die Fruchtbarkeit eines christlichen Interpretationsatzes testen. Als biblisches Muster für die zweiaktige Werkstruktur bietet sich die Einteilung der Heiligen Schrift in Altes and Neues Testament an, auf deren Basis Joachim von Fiore im Hochmittelalter eine spekulative Geschichtslehre entwickelt hatte. Aus diesen mit Gottvater und Jesus in Beziehung gesetzten Epochen extrapolierte Joachim von Fiore, vom Trinitätsgedanken gelietet, ein kommendes, drittes Reich, das Reich des Heiligen Geistes, das Reich der Hoffnung. Beckett, der Joachim kannte und von derartigen Zahlenspielen fasziniert war ... könnte mit *Waiting for Godot* also einen ironischen Kommentar zur naiv-progressistischen Geschichtauffassung des Kalabreser Abtes intendiert haben" (*Die Kunst der Paradoxie: Sinnsuche und Scheitern bei Samuel Beckett* [München: Wilhelm Fink Verlag, 1976], pp. 127-28. See also my "The Advents of Godot," *Religion in Life* 42 (Summer 1973): 168-78.

Chapter 4

1. For various religious interpretations of this play see Josephine Jacobsen and William Mueller, *The Testament of Samuel Beckett* (New York: Hill and Wang, 1964); V. A. Kolve, "Religious Language in *Waiting for Godot*," *Centennial Review* 11 (Winter 1967): 102-27; Charles McCoy, "*Waiting for Godot:* A Biblical Appraisal," *Religion in Life* 28 (Fall 1959): 595-643; and Nathan Scott, *Samuel Beckett* (New York: Hillary House, 1965).

2. Wylie Sypher, *Loss of the Self in Modern Literature and Art* (New York: Random House, 1962), p. 157. On this question of Pozzo as Godot see also C. Chadwick, "*Waiting for Godot:* A Logical Approach," *Symposium* 14 (Winter 1960): 255; Ronald Gray, "*Waiting for Godot:* A Christian Interpretation," *Listener* 57 (January 24, 1957): 160-61; and Jean Onimus, *Beckett* (Paris: Desclée de Brouwer, 1968). On the same note Gerhart Hauptmann wrote what he thought was his greatest work, *Till Eulenspiegel,* in which God appears as "Gott Barnum-Saturn," a creature of frightening, fraudulent propensities — just like Pozzo. Edmund Wilson has given a curious portrait of a monstrous Messiah in his chapter on the Jews in *A Piece of My Mind* (New York: Allen, 1957), pp. 82-103.

3. Samuel Beckett, *Poèmes, Les Temps Modernes,* no. 14 (Nov.

1946), p. 290. See also Lawrence Harvey, *Samuel Beckett, Poet and Critic* (Princeton, N. J.: Princeton University Press, 1970), pp. 192-93.
  4. Edgar Hennecke, *New Testament Apocrypha* (Philadelphia: Westminster Press, 1963), 1:286. See also Montague Rhodes James, *The Apocryphal New Testament* (Oxford: Oxford University Press, 1924).
  5. See Bradbrook, *Literature in Action,* p. 20. On the dog theme see Erica Ostrovsky, "Le Silence de Babel," in the *Cahier Samuel Beckett* (Paris: Editions de l'Herne, 1976), pp. 209-10.
  6. Samuel Beckett, *Molloy* (New York: Grove Press, 1970), p. 72. According to Richard Ellmann, "Joyce took great interest in the flower, Moly, which enables Odysseus to thwart the wiles of Circe and keep her from turning him into a pig. Joyce consulted many friends about Moly, and finally wrote Budgen his decision, which proved more inclusive than exclusive: 'Moly is the gift of Hermes, god of public ways, and is the invisible influence (prayer, chance, agility, *presence of mind,* power of recuperation which saves in case of accident. This would cover immunity from syphilis ... swine-love?" (*Ulysses on the Liffey* [New York: Oxford University Press, 1972], pp. 145-46). Considering the references to venereal diseases in the play, it is interesting to consider Didi's stage business — his way of walking, his unspecified ailment which obliges him to make trips offstage. Perhaps Vladimir's other name is derived from epididymitis, the pain from which, according to C. F. Marshall, "varies considerably, and is not always proportionate to the degree of swelling of the testi- cle. Sometimes the pain radiates to the loins or down the thighs; it is always increased by walking, and the patient adopts a bent attitude, with the thighs everted" (*Syphilis and Venereal Diseases* [New York: William Word, 1921], p. 383). With reference to Beckett's character it is relevant to acknowledge that the Greek word didymus also signi- fies "testicle." For more details on genital symbolism and onomastic techniques in this play see note 17 in this chapter.
  7. C. J. S. Thompson writes about the mandrake: "Hildegard tells us that it was fashioned out of the same earth whereof God created Adam, and that its likeness to man is the wile of the devil which dis- tinguishes it above all other plants" (*The Mystic Mandrake* [London: Rider & Co., 1934], p. 24). On the religious significance of this plant see John Allegro, *The Sacred Mushroom* (New York: Doubleday, 1970). See also Hugh Rahner, *Greek Myths and Christian Mysteries* (New York: Harper & Row, 1963), pp. 179-277.
  8. Albert-Marie Schmidt, *La Mandragore* (Paris: Flammarion, 1958),

p. 52. Regarding Gogo's names, it is interesting to note that he also answers to "Catulle" in the French version. Perhaps Beckett had in mind the Roman poet of satiric and erotic verse, or perhaps he was evoking the name of a lesser-known mime-writer of the first century who composed a play, *Laureolus,* in which the crucifixion of a bandit or thief was depicted. Concerning the religious significance of Beckett's character names, perhaps Didi is derived from Didier. There was a Saint Didier who, during the persecutions of Diocletian, was beheaded at Pozzuoli. See also Pilling, *Samuel Beckett,* p. 119.

9. See also E. S. Drower, *The Secret Adam: A Study of Nasorean Gnosis* (Oxford: Oxford University Press, 1960); R. M. Grant, *Gnosticism and Early Christianity* (New York: Columbia University Press, 1959); Robin Scroggs, *The Last Adam: A Study in Pauline Anthropology* (Philadelphia: Westminster Press, 1966); and R. M. Wilson, *Gnosis and the New Testament* (Oxford: Oxford University Press, 1968).

10. This ancient world view did not die out like so many other exotic heresies. In his seminal work on the subject Hans Jonas writes: "Yet in one way or another Marcionitism has remained an issue in Christianity to this day" (*The Gnostic Religion* [Boston: Beacon Press, 1958], p. 146).

11. For a detailed discussion of Beckett's use of the Cain and Abel myth see Bert O. States, *Shape of Paradox,* pp. 9-31. The Cain-Abel pun was one that Joyce, too, found difficult to resist. See Glasheen, *Second Census of Finnegan's Wake,* pp. 44-45; and Hélène Cixous, *Prénoms de personne* (Paris: Seuil, 1974), p. 313. Per Nykrog observes that Balzac's diabolical Vautrin claimed to be both Cain and Abel in his *La Pensée de Balzac* (Copenhagen: Munksgaard, 1965), pp. 366-87. For an analysis of the use of paradoxical language, see Sigmund Freud, "The Antithetical Sense of Primal Words," in *Collected Papers,* trans. Joan Rivière (London: Hogarth Press, 1953), 4:185-91. See also Wladimir Granoff, *Filiations: l'avenir du complexe d'Oedipe* (Paris: Editions de Minuit, 1975), pp. 410-29.

12. Jean-Paul Sartre, *Being and Nothingness,* trans. Hazel E. Barnes, (New York: Philosophical Library, 1956), p. 162.

13. A present-day descendant of this famous family, a Catholic layman named Olivier Pozzo di Borgo, has taken to attacking what he terms Zionism. See Léon Poliakov, *De l'antisionisme à l'antisémitisme* (Calmann-Levy, 1969), p. 160; and Emile Lavielle, *En Attendant Godot de Beckett* (Paris: Hachette, 1970), p. 40.

14. Hugh Kenner, *Samuel Beckett: A Critical Study* (Berkeley:

University of California Press, 1968), p. 39. See Giuseppina Restivo, "Pozzo e Joyce," *Studi Inglesi* 2 (1975): 275-82. John Fletcher examines the influence of Dante on Beckett in "The Debt to Dante," without, however, referring to the significance of the term *pozzo* (*Samuel Beckett's Art* [London: Chatto & Windus, 1967], p. 106).

15. Raymond Federman and John Fletcher, *Samuel Beckett: His Works and His Critics* (Berkeley: University of California Press, 1970), p. 5. See also Voltaire, *Candide* (Paris: Hachette, 1913), p. 64.

16. Denis Diderot, *Le Neveu de Rameau* (Paris: Gallimard, Pléiade, 1957), p. 469.

17. Whatever Beckett's knowledge of Yiddish or Russian may be, there is in these languages a pungent term (*potz*) to describe this part of the anatomy which perfectly reflects and sounds like Pozzo's name. In the same vein the nominal linkage of the divine and the obscene has been recognized in the Shakespearean expression "cock's passion" by Eric Partridge, who writes: "Here, *cock* is a euphemism for *God*" [London: Routledge & Kegan Paul, 1955], p. 88). See also Margaret Solomon, *Eternal Geometer: The Sexual Universe of Finnegans Wake* (Carbondale: Southern Illinois University Press, 1969), p. ix; and Ihab Hassan, *Paracriticisms* (Urbana: University of Illinois Press, 1975), pp. 87-88. It is possible that Pozzo's name was derived from the model of one of Proust's characters, (Dr. Cottard) who was known as Dr. Pozzi, "was talkative, hollow and reeking of hair oil," and whose wife was called "Pozzi's mute." See George D. Painter, *Proust: The Early Years* (Boston: Little, Brown, 1959), pp. 125-26.

18. To appreciate the profound implications of this radical shift in Christian thinking see Hans Frei, *The Eclipse of Biblical Narrative: A Study in Eighteenth and Nineteenth Century Hermeneutics* (New Haven, Conn: Yale University Press, 1974); and Wilhelm Pauck, *Harnack and Troeltsch: Two Historical Theologians* (New York: Oxford University Press, 1968).

19. Ruth Wisse writes perceptively about the literary comic figure of the schlemiel as being committed to a philosophy of "as if," of the clown given to a world view of radical irony, contingency, and absurdity. See *The Schlemiel as Modern Hero* (Chicago: University of Chicago Press, 1971), p. 65.

20. Gershom Scholem, *The Messianic Idea in Judaism* (New York: Schocken Books, 1971), p. 13. See also his *Sabbatai Sevi: The Mystical Messiah* (Princeton, N. J.: Princeton University Press, 1973); and Joseph Klausner, *The Messianic Idea in Israel* (London: George Allen and Unwin, 1956). On the question of Jewish reluctance to accept salva-

tion, see Jacqueline Genot-Bismuth's comments on the playwright Haim Hazaz, "Le Dualité du temps humain dans *Au Terme des Jours*," in her *La Mort de Godot* (Paris: Lettres Modernes, 1970), p. 151. In his observations on the radical malaise in Western culture, George Steiner echoes the apocalyptic message in Judaism: "Three times, Judaism produced a summons to perfection and sought to impose it on the current and currency of western life. Deep loathing built up in the social unconscious, murderous resentments" (*In Bluebeard's Castle* [New Haven, Conn.: Yale University Press, 1971], p. 45.

21. Hugh Kenner, *A Reader's Guide to Samuel Beckett* (New York: Farrar, Straus & Giroux, 1973), p. 30.

22. On Beckett's sense of dramatic balance John Fletcher writes: "Not symmetry, therefore, but asymmetry is essential to drive home the point being made in *Godot* about the hopelessness of the ever-renewed wait, but to avoid clumsy obviousness the roles are reassigned" ("Studies in Variations on the Permitted Lie," *Forces in Modern French Drama* [New York: Frederick Ungar, 1972], p. 199.

23. See Eugene Webb, *The Dark Dove* (Seattle: University of Washington Press, 1975).

24. Israel Shenker, "Moody Man of Letters," *New York Times,* May 6, 1956.

Chapter 5

1. Eva Metman, "Reflections on Samuel Beckett's Plays," *Journal of Analytical Psychology* 5 (January, 1960): 41-63. For a more detailed analysis incorporating Jungian interpretation, see Sighle Kennedy, *Murphy's Bed: A Study of Real Sources and Sur-real Associations in Samuel Beckett's First Novel,* (Lewisburg, Pa.: Bucknell University Press, 1971), pp. 237-43.

2. G. C. Barnard, *Samuel Beckett,* p. 89. For a detailed analysis of schizophrenia in art, see John Vernon, *The Garden and the Map* (Urbana: University of Illinois Press, 1973).

3. Eugene Webb, *The Plays of Samuel Beckett* (Seattle: University of Washington Press, 1972), p. 29.

4. David Hesla, *The Shape of Chaos: An Interpretation of the Art of Samuel Beckett* (Minneapolis: University of Minnesota Press, 1971), p. 200. With Pozzo and Lucky in mind, Hesla comments on Hegel's portrait of master and slave: "Hence the slave must create his master and sustain him in his mastery, and this of course means that the slave is master of the master, and this is no slavery at all" (p. 195). This view

falls somewhat short of considering the dialectical transformation of roles as exemplified by the pantomime and hat-exchange routine. The relationship between Pozzo and Lucky (and Gogo and Didi) appears to be the most exquisite of all forms of slavery in that they are still bound to each other. Stanley Rosen writes in this regard: "We come ... to the crucial transpositon in the master-slave relation, which is an excellent illustration of the dialectic of the inverted world. As that upon which the master depends, the slave comes to recognize his own independence, and precisely as dependent. Each is the opposite of himself; each is implicitly the other. We see here with great clarity how the master and the slave are related as position and negation, or identity and difference" (*G. W. F. Hegel* [New Haven: Yale University Press, 1974], p. 162. See also Murray Greene, "Hegel's 'Unhappy Consciousness' and Nietzsche's 'Slave Morality,'" in *Hegel and the Philosophy of Religion,* ed. Darrel Christensen (The Hague: Martinus Nijhoff, 1970), pp. 125-41; and Jean Hyppolite, *Genèse et structure de la Phénoménologie de l'Esprit de Hegel* (Paris: Aubier, 1946), 1:166.

5. For a similar development in Joyce, see Saul Field and Morton Levitt, *Bloomsday* (Greenwich, Conn.: New York Graphic Society, 1972), p. 54.

6. For a detailed analysis of this psychological problem, see Herbert Fingaretti, *Self-Deception* (London: Routledge & Kegan Paul, 1969), p. 137.

7. See in particular Sigmund Freud, "Splitting of the Ego in the Defensive Process," in his *Collected Papers,* 5:372-75.

8. Jean-Paul Sartre, *Being and Nothingness* (New York: Philosophical Library, 1956), pp. 46-70. See also Martin Esslin, *Theater of the Absurd,* p. 43.

9. See R. D. Laing, *The Divided Self* (New York: Pantheon, 1960).

10. Beckett's notion about dealing with nothingness as if it were something was developed by the German philosopher Hans Vaihinger whose chief work, *Die Philosophie des Als Ob* (Leipzig: Meiner, 1911), investigates the concept of fiction as the basis of thinking and art. Vaihinger was much influenced by Nietzsche, whose illuminating passages in *The Antichrist* on self-deception herald those of Freud and Sartre. See also Maria Bindschedler, *Nietzsche und die Poetische Lüge* (Berlin: De Gruyter, 1966).

11. On the radical differences distinguishing these two philosophers, see Giorgio de Santillana, "Vico and Descartes," in his *Reflections on Men and Ideas* (Cambridge: M.I.T. Press, 1968), pp. 206-18.

12. For Beckett's references to Heraclitus and Democritus, see John Fletcher, *Samuel Beckett's Art,* pp. 121-37.

13. Samuel Beckett, *Proust,* p. 47.

14. Quoted by Alec Reid, *All I Can Manage More than I Could* (New York: Grove Press, 1971), p. 11.

15. Concerning the importance of the commedia in reflecting reality and illusion, especially in Antonioni's film *Blow-Up,* see Andrew Sarris, *Confessions of a Cultist: On the Cinema, 1955 – 1969* (New York: Simon & Schuster, 1970), p. 284. On the significance of multiple literary interpretations, see Harold Bloom, *A Map of Misreading* (New York: Oxford University Press, 1975).

16. Hugh Kenner, *The Stoic Comedians* (Boston: Beacon, 1962), pp. 97, 106.

17. Kenner, *Samuel Beckett,* p. 204.

18. On the significance of God's many names in the works of James Joyce, see Hélène Cixous, *Prénoms de Personne,* pp. 260-63.

19. Samuel Beckett, *Our Exagmination,* p. 3.

20. Lawrence Harvey, *Samuel Beckett, Poet and Critic,* p. 434. See also J. L. Styan's perceptive comments on the ambivalent theater of Beckett in *The Dark Comedy* (Cambridge, England: Cambridge University Press, 1968), p. 233.

21. In a similar line of interpretation Vivian Mercier writes: "If Pozzo is Godot and Godot is God, we get a Viconian cycle, in which history repeats itself every evening. The Incarnation (of the Second Coming) is constantly re-enacted, always with the same result. Godot is not rejected; he simply passes unrecognized because his attributes are so completely out of harmony with the aspirations of those who wait for him" ("Pyrrhonian Eclogue," p. 623). This argument could be enhanced by affirming that while Pozzo does fulfill this role he also suggests by the assonance of his name an affinity with Gogo which stresses the reversed parts between pairs. This is the basic truth which Didi prefers to overlook. C. Chadwick also reasons thus: "Surely a logical argument, without any *a priori* assumptions, must run as follows: Godot is God, Pozzo is Godot, Pozzo is therefore God and since Pozzo is nothing but a tyrant and a slavedriver so too is God" (*"Waiting for Godot:* A Logical Approach," *Symposium* 14 (Winter 1960): 255). The views of these two distinguished critics are on the right track but they do not go far enough. By ignoring the play-within-the-play they do not see that Beckett intends to present something more than an indirectly horrific image of God. As Chadwick suggests, the assonance between Pozzo's and Godot's names hints at a common identity for

these two characters, but this observation is not extended to Gogo or to the similarity between Didi and Lucky. By linking and reversing these roles Beckett intimates not so much that God as Pozzo is a monster who comes from afar and arrives unrecognized, but rather that the despotism comes from within the primal couple and is reflected in Gogo. The real tyranny is that of the imagination. Didi is his own prisoner and victim, and he wishes he could ignore this intuition.

22. That Beckett's work ultimately turns toward this view of humanity's endless wandering is evidenced in a recent example of his prose, "Se Voir": "Au-delà de la fosse il n'y a rien. On le sait puisqu'il faut le dire. Arène étendue noire. Des millions peuvent s'y tenir. Errants et immobiles. Sans jamais se toucher. C'est tout ce qu'on sait" (*Pour finir encore et autres foirades* [Paris: Editions de Minuit, 1976], p. 51).

BIBLIOGRAPHY

Only a selection of works consulted in this study is listed below. For detailed bibliographies on Beckett see Raymond Federman and John Fletcher, *Samuel Beckett: His Works and His Critics* (Berkeley: University of California Press, 1970); and *Samuel Beckett I: Calepins de Bibliographie,* ed. Jackson R. Bryer (Paris: Lettres Modernes, Minard, 1972). For a concise bibliography of criticism up to 1968, see Jackson R. Bryer's "Samuel Beckett: A Checklist of Criticism" in *Samuel Beckett Now,* ed. Melvin J. Friedman (Chicago: University of Chicago Press, 1970).

Works of Beckett

"Dante ... Bruno . Vico .. Joyce," in *Our Exagmination Round His Factification for Incamination of Work in Progress.* London: Faber and Faber, 1961.
En Attendant Godot. Paris: Editions de Minuit, 1952.
Endgame. New York: Grove Press, 1957.
Mercier et Camier. Paris: Editions de Minuit, 1970.
Molloy. New York: Grove Press, 1970.
Malone Dies. New York: Grove Press, 1956.
More Pricks than Kicks. New York: Grove Press, 1972.
Murphy. New York: Grove Press, 1957.
Pour finir encore et autres foirades. Paris: Editions de Minuit, 1976.
Proust. New York: Grove Press, 1957.
Stories and Texts for Nothing. New York: Grove Press, 1967.
Waiting for Godot. New York: Grove Press, 1954.
Watt. New York: Grove Press, 1970.

Studies on Beckett

Abbott, H. Porter. *The Fiction of Samuel Beckett: Form and Effect.* Berkeley: University of California Press, 1973.

Abel, Lionel. *Metatheatre: A New View of Dramatic Form.* New York: Hill and Wang, 1963.

Adorno, Theodor W. "Versuch, das Endspiel zu verstehen," in *Noten zur Literatur, II.* Frankfurt am Main: Suhrkamp Verlag, 1961.

Alvarez, Alfred. *Samuel Beckett.* New York: Viking, 1973.

Bair, Deirdre. *Samuel Beckett: A Biography.* New York: Harcourt Brace Jovanovich, 1978.

Barnard, G. C. *Samuel Beckett, A New Approach: A Study of the Novels and Plays.* New York: Dodd, Mead, 1970.

Bentley, Eric. *The Theater of Commitment and Other Essays on Drama in Our Society.* New York: Atheneum, 1967.

Bernal, Olga. *Langage et fiction dans le roman de Beckett.* Paris: Gallimard, 1969.

Bersani, Leo. *Balzac to Beckett: Center and Circumference in French Fiction.* New York: Oxford University Press, 1970.

Birkenhauer, Klaus. *Samuel Beckett.* Hamburg: Rowohlt, 1972.

Bishop, Tom, and Federman, Raymond, eds. *Samuel Beckett.* Paris: Cahier de l'Herne, 1976.

Bowles, Patrick. "How Samuel Beckett Sees the Universe." *Listener* 59 (June 6, 1958): 1011.

Breuer, Horst. *Samuel Beckett: Lernpsychologie und leibliche Determination.* Munich: Fink Verlag, 1972.

Breuer, Rolf. *Die Kunst der Paradoxie: Sinnsuche und Scheitern bei Samuel Beckett.* Munich: Fink Verlag, 1976.

Brooke-Rose, Christine. "Samuel Beckett and the Anti-Novel." *London Magazine* 5 (December 1958): 38-46.

Brunel, Pierre. *La Mort de Godot.* Paris: Lettres Modernes, Minard, 1970.

Busi, Frederick. "The Advents of Godot." *Religion in Life* 42 (Summer 1973): 168-78.

——. "Naming Day in No-Man's Land: Samuel Beckett's Use of Names in *Waiting for Godot.*" *Boston University Journal* Winter 1974, 20-29.

——. "*Waiting for Godot: A Modern Don Quixote?*" *Hispania* 57 (1974): 876-85.

——. "Joycean Echoes in *Waiting for Godot.*" *Research Studies* 43 (June 1975): 71-87.

——. "Cervantes's Use of Character Names and the *Commedia dell' Arte.*" *Romance Notes* 17 (Spring 1977): 314-19.

Calder, John, ed. *Beckett at 60.* London: Calder and Boyars, 1967.

Chadwick, C. "*Waiting for Godot:* A Logical Approach." *Symposium* 14 (1960): 252-57.

Champigny, Robert. "Interprétation de *En attendant Godot.*" *PMLA* 75 (1960): 329-31.

Closs, August. "Formprobleme und Möglichkeiten zur Gestaltung der Tragödie in der Gegenwart." *Stil-und Formprobleme* 5 (1960): 483-91.

Coe, Richard. *Samuel Beckett.* New York: Grove Press, 1970.

Cohn, Ruby. *Samuel Beckett: The Comic Gamut.* New Brunswick, N. J.: Rutgers University Press, 1962.

———, ed. *Casebook on "Waiting for Godot."* New York: Grove Press, 1967.

———. *Back to Beckett.* Princeton, N. J.: Princeton University Press, 1973.

———, ed. *Samuel Beckett: A Collection of Criticism.* New York: McGraw-Hill, 1975.

Croussy, Guy. *Beckett.* Paris: Hachette, 1971.

Doherty, Francis. *Samuel Beckett.* London: Hutchinson University Library, 1971.

Duckworth, Colin. *Angels of Darkness: Dramatic Effect in Beckett and Ionesco.* New York: Barnes and Noble, 1972.

Dukore, Bernard F. "The Other Pair in *Waiting for Godot.*" *Drama Survey* 7 (1969): 133-37.

Durozoi, Gérard. *Beckett.* Paris: Bordas, 1972.

Egebak, Niels. *Beckett Palimpsest.* Copenhagen: Arena, 1969.

Esslin, Martin. *The Theatre of the Absurd.* New York: Anchor Books, 1969.

Federman, Raymond. *Journey to Chaos: Samuel Beckett's Early Fiction.* Berkeley: University of California Press, 1965.

———. "Beckettian Paradox: Who Is Telling the Truth?" in *Samuel Beckett Now,* edited by Melvin J. Friedman. Chicago: University of Chicago Press, 1970.

Findlay, Robert. "Confrontation in Waiting: *Godot* and the Wakefield Play." *Renascence* 21 (1969): 195-202.

Fletcher, John. *The Novels of Samuel Beckett.* New York: Barnes and Noble, 1964.

———. *Samuel Beckett's Art.* London: Chatto and Windus, 1967.

———. "The Arrival of Godot." *Modern Language Review* 37 (October 1969): 34-48.

———. *Forces in Modern French Drama.* New York: Ungar, 1972.

———, and Sperling, John. *Beckett: A Study of His Plays.* New York: Hill and Wang, 1972.

Foucré, Michèle. *Le Geste et la parole dans le théâtre de Samuel Beckett.* Paris: Nizet, 1970.

Gessner, Niklaus. *Die Unzulänglichkeit der Sprache: Eine Untersuchung*

über Formzerfall und Beziehungslosigkeit bei Samuel Beckett.
Zurich: Juris Verlag, 1957.

Gray, Ronald. *"Waiting for Godot:* A Christian Interpretation." *Listener*
57 (24 January 1957): 160-61.

Grossvogel, David I. *The Blasphemers: The Theater of Brecht, Ionesco,
Beckett, Genet.* Ithaca, N. Y.: Cornell University Press, 1966.

Harvey, Lawrence E. *Samuel Beckett, Poet and Critic.* Princeton, N. J.:
Princeton University Press, 1970.

Hassan, Ihab. *The Literature of Silence: Henry Miller and Samuel
Beckett.* New York: Knopf, 1967.

———. *The Dismemberment of Orpheus: Toward a Post-Modern Literature.* New York: Oxford University Press, 1971.

———. *Paracriticisms: Seven Speculations of the Times.* Urbana: University of Illinois Press, 1975.

Hensel, Georg. *Samuel Beckett.* Hannover: Friedrich Verlag, 1968.

Hesla, David. *The Shape of Chaos: An Interpretation of the Art of
Samuel Beckett.* Minneapolis: University of Minnesota Press, 1971.

Hoffman, Frederick John. *Samuel Beckett: The Language of Self.*
Carbondale: Southern Illinois University Press, 1962.

Hubert, Renée Riese. "The Couple and the Performance in Samuel
Beckett's Plays." *L'Esprit Créateur* 2 (1962): 177.

Jacobsen, Josephine, and Mueller, William R. *The Testament of Samuel
Beckett.* New York: Hill and Wang, 1964.

Janvier, Ludovic. *Pour Samuel Beckett.* Paris: Editions de Minuit, 1966.

———. *Samuel Beckett par lui-même.* Paris: Seuil, 1969.

Kennedy, Sighle. *Murphy's Bed: A Study of Real Sources and Sur-Real
Associations in Samuel Beckett's First Novel.* Lewisburg, Pa.:
Bucknell University Press, 1971.

Kenner, Hugh. *Flaubert, Joyce, and Beckett: The Stoic Comedians.*
Boston: Beacon, 1962.

———. *Samuel Beckett: A Critical Study.* Berkeley: University of
California Press, 1968.

———. *A Reader's Guide to Samuel Beckett.* New York: Farrar, Straus
and Giroux, 1973.

Kern, Edith G. "Drama Stripped for Inaction: Beckett's *Godot.*" *Yale
French Studies* 14 (Winter 1954-55): 41-47.

———. "Beckett and the Spirit of the Commedia dell' Arte." *Modern
Drama* 9 (1966): 260.

———. *Existential Thought and Fictional Technique: Kierkegaard, Sartre,
Beckett.* New Haven: Yale University Press, 1970.

Knowlson, James. *Light and Darkness in the Theater of Samuel Beckett.*
London: Turret Books, 1972.

Kolve, V. A. "Religious Language in *Waiting for Godot.*" *Centennial Review* 11 (Winter 1967): 102-27.

Lalande, Bernard. *"En Attendant Godot": Beckett.* Paris: Hatier, 1970.

Lavielle, Emile. *"En Attendant Godot" de Beckett.* Paris: Hachette, 1973.

Leventhal, A. J. "The Beckett Hero." In *Samuel Beckett: A Collection of Critical Essays,* edited by Martin Esslin. Englewood Cliffs, N.J.: Prentice-Hall, 1965.

Marissel, André. *Samuel Beckett.* Paris: Editions Universitaires, 1963.

Mayoux, Jean-Jacques. "Beckett and Expressionism." Translated by Ruby Cohn. *Modern Drama* 9 (1966): 238-41.

McCoy, Charles. *"Waiting for Godot:* A Biblical Appraisal." *Religion in Life* 28 (1959): 595-603.

Mélèse, Pierre. *Samuel Beckett.* Paris: Seghers, 1966.

Mercier, Vivian. "A Pyrrhonian Eclogue." *Hudson Review* 7 (1955): 620-24.

——. *Beckett/Beckett.* New York: Oxford University Press, 1977.

Metman, Eva. "Reflections on Samuel Beckett's Plays." *Journal of Analytical Psychology* 5 (January 1960): 41-63.

Miller, Walter James, and Nelson, Bonnie. *Samuel Beckett's "Waiting for Godot."* New York: Monarch Press, 1971.

Moore, John R. "A Farewell to Something." *Tulane Drama Review* 5 (September 1960): 49-60.

Murray, Patrick. *Samuel Beckett.* Cork: Mercier Press, 1970.

Newlove, Donald. Review of *First Love and Other Stories. Village Voice,* 12 October 1974, p. 31.

Norès, Dominique. *Beckett.* Paris: Garnier, 1971.

Oliva, Renato. *Samuel Beckett.* Milan: Mursia, 1967.

Onimus, Jean. *Beckett.* Paris: Desclée de Brouwer, 1968.

Perche, Louis. *Beckett.* Paris: Editions du Centurion, 1969.

Pilling, John. *Samuel Beckett.* London: Routledge and Kegan Paul, 1976.

Reid, Alec. *All I Can Manage More than I Could: An Approach to the Plays of Samuel Beckett.* New York: Grove Press, 1971.

Restivo, Giuseppina, "Pozzo e Joyce," *Studi Inglesi,* 2 (1975): 275-82.

Robbe-Grillet, Alain. *For A New Novel.* Translated by Richard Howard. New York: Grove Press, 1965.

Robinson, Michael. *The Long Sonata of the Dead: A Study of Samuel Beckett.* New York: Grove Press, 1969.

Rojtman, Betty. *Forme et signification dans le théâtre de Beckett.* Paris: Nizet, 1976.

Rosen, Steven J. *Samuel Beckett and the Pessimistic Tradition.* New Brunswick, N.J.: Rutgers University Press, 1977.

Saint-Martin, Fernande. *Samuel Beckett et l'univers de la fiction.* Montréal: Les Presses de l'Université de Montréal, 1976.

Scarry, E. M. "Six Ways To Kill a Blackbird or Any Other Intentional Object: Samuel Beckett's Method of Meaning." *James Joyce Quarterly* 8 (1971): 278-89.

Schlossberg, Edwin. *Einstein and Beckett: A Record of an Imaginary Discussion with Albert Einstein and Samuel Beckett.* New York: Links Books, 1973.

Schoell, Konrad. *Das Theater Samuel Becketts.* Munich: Fink Verlag, 1967.

Scott, Nathan A. *Samuel Beckett.* New York: Hillary House, 1965.

Sheedy, John. "The Net." In *Casebook on Waiting for Godot,* edited by Ruby Cohn, pp. 159-66. New York: Grove Press, 1967.

Shenker, Israel. "Moody Man of Letters." *New York Times,* 6 May 1956.

Sherzer, Dina. *Structure de la trilogie de Beckett.* The Hague: Mouton, 1976.

States, Bert O. *The Shape of Paradox: An Essay on "Waiting for Godot."* Berkeley: University of California Press, 1978.

Sypher, Wylie. *Loss of the Self in Modern Literature and Art.* New York: Random House, 1962.

Szanto, George H. "Samuel Beckett: Dramatic Possibilities." *Massachusetts Review* 15 (1974): 735-61.

Tagliaferri, Aldo. *Beckett e l'iperdeterminazione Letteraria.* Milan: Feltrinelli, 1967.

Taylor, Andrew. "The Minimal Affirmation of Godot." *Critical Review* 12 (1969): 3-14.

Webb, Eugene. *The Plays of Samuel Beckett.* Seattle: University of Washington Press, 1972.

——. "Pozzo in Bloomsbury: A Possible Allusion to Beckett's *Waiting for Godot." Journal of Modern Literature* 5 (1976): 326-31.

Worth, Katharine, ed. *Beckett the Shape Changer: A Symposium.* London: Routledge and Kegan Paul, 1975.

INDEX